THE SENSITIVE

THE SENSITIVE MANIPULATOR

The change agent who builds with others

William G. Dyer

Brigham Young University Press   Provo, Utah

Library of Congress Catalog Card Number: 72-80277
International Standard Book Number: 0-8425-1477-5
Brigham Young University Press, Provo, Utah 84601
© 1972 by Brigham Young University Press. All rights reserved
Printed in the United States of America
72 5M 3452

The cruelest lies are often told in silence.
Robert Louis Stevenson

Contents

*Articles marked with an asterisk were previously published in journals. They have been revised to fit the format of this book.

I am by temperament, socialization, and inclination, an idealist and a "helper." By profession I am an applied behavioral scientist and a professional consultant and change agent. My values and goals move me to keep trying to help people and organizations and society become better, somehow. Somewhere deep in me is the conviction that yearnings and strivings for something finer in performance are characteristics of all men until and unless something or someone stunts those desires or causes them to die. An almost unpardonable sin, to me, is to be a "killer of the dreams" in others.

Like many, I have been strongly influenced by the writings and life of Abraham Maslow and also Jack Gibb and then Chris Argyris, Douglas McGregor, Rensis Likert, Kurt Lewin, and Carl Rogers among many. I think that people are motivated by a desire to become "self-actualized"—to somehow be the best they can be. This best is represented by human behavior that has been called *authentic* or *congruent* and refers to that sublime human condition when a person is finally capable of behaving in ways that represent his best intentions, values, ideals, and feelings. Thus I begin this volume of writings with two sections on what could be called the *goals of personal change*: authenticity and congruence in behavior.

These writings are a collection of articles that I have written through the years in an attempt to explain and describe the essentials of personal and organizational change. The overriding theme centers on helping others to change in directions of improved maturity, effectiveness, and satisfaction. Some of these writings are concerned with individual change, some with the conditions in a relationship that affects those involved, and some with the nature of the total organization—a system that shapes the behavior of its members. Still another set of these articles deals with the role of the person who chooses to become an agent for change, to spend his career life working for individual, group, and organizational improvement.

Many of the articles draw upon the family as a basic context for illustrating the principle or dimension under discussion. I have used the family framework deliberately for the following reasons:

1. I hope to influence parents so they will begin to initiate change in their own family systems. The family still remains the primary social system that provides the nurturance for the healthy development of the human personality. If we can change the family, there is hope for changing other parts of our larger society.

2. The family is the one system that everyone understands. If I were to use business, education, religion, or government examples, I feel I would lead some into foreign territory, but the family should be common ground for almost everyone.

3. Many people plan change in the areas of their occupations or professional careers. I hope to have them think of *planning* for change in their families as well. The manager of the business firm is also a husband and a father. If he can achieve more consistent success in his family roles, I feel he will be freer and have more energy to also pursue success in his profession. A wise man once said, "No success can compensate for failure in the home."

4. For most women, the home is the dominant system, and the rearing of children the most important product. I would like to influence the women who may read this volume to stimulate them to be more effective agents for change within their own homes.

If we are to achieve personal growth, I feel that it is essential that the human organizations that are the hewers and molders of human performance be shaped and more fitly fashioned. Some systems (family, school, church, and work) beat and bludgeon, scream and stamp until they force into their mold something that resembles the desired human resultant. Other systems fashion with finesse, with skill and sensitivity, the human factor until it grows and develops into a wondrous achievement. I have tried to cover the elements of the interpersonal scene that impact upon the individual, and such critical conditions as trust, communication, interdependence, group life, and motivation are examined.

I frequently use the terms growth and change as synonyms in the book. People change as they grow (and often vice versa, but sometimes not). Change is considered in the framework of planning, for planned change is the great concern — seeing the end from the beginning. And, like a builder or painter who has a vision of his creation in his mind's eye, collects and assembles and arranges all of the necessary materials and then works carefully to add, reduce, shape, and mold those needed ingredients until the final reality is a thrilling representation of the vision — so also is a human architect. But any creation has its inconsistencies, its problems or concerns, and the second section in the volume deals with some of those conditions that arise to make human growth a constant challenge. Sometimes change is easily accepted and dramatic in its impact for growth. At other times a change attempt is stubbornly resisted and feeble in its effect. Why this is represents another part of the continuous challenge. Perhaps an important ingredient or element is missing in the change strategy, the change action, or the performance of the change agent. One section of the volume deals with the work of the person who defines his role as one who wants to bring about improvement. These writings try to help him look at his diagnostic skills, his role as a change agent, his ability to deal effectively with individuals, groups, and larger systems.

One may find it more fruitful to read this volume selectively. Many who are concerned about the matter of change are not professional change agents or consultants, but as parents, teachers, managers, and organization leaders they may want to consider the element of change and introspect to see if their attempts at improvement include the conditions described here. The section on barriers to change discusses certain conditions that deter people from achieving change goals. These are forces that confront both the professional who is helping others and the individual concerned with his own growth.

The final section of this volume is directed toward the person who sees the helping or change relationship as a major part of his personal career. While written for the professional consultants or change agents, other nonprofessionals, such as teachers, managers, ministers, and even parents, may see in this section certain orientations that will be helpful to the change-directed aspects of their jobs.

Through the years, many have provided the stimulation that has prompted these writings. I wish to particularly acknowledge the major influence of Jack Gibb who perhaps more than any single person has helped shape my thinking and move me along my career path. For many years my association with the network of the NTL Institute of Applied Behavioral Science has been a major force in my own personal and professional growth. Without any doubt the greatest single laboratory for trying out my own change ideas has been my family, and to these magnificent subjects — Bonnie, Gibb, Mike, Lisa, Jeff, and David — I express my eternal love. Hopefully the spirit of growth and change will be a personal challenge for them, too.

Finally I would like to express appreciation for the excellent support and assistance given by Gail W. Bell of the Brigham Young University Press who has helped wonderfully in shaping this volume into a finished product.

Change will occur whether we like it, plan it, or try to ignore it. Perhaps the most constant process we know about is change: All individuals and organizations change. It may come slowly and subtly or be rapid and dramatic, but change will occur. The critical issue is: Can we plan the change so that it moves in the direction we desire and at a rate we control.

Planned change is a fundamental goal for people and organizations. Many individuals would like to define a direction for their own development, set goals for personal improvement, and achieve the satisfaction that comes from seeing themselves gain greater personal maturity, an expansion of talents, and a widening of perspective or effectiveness. While such personal change is desired by many, it is an elusive condition. The forces that impede or facilitate change are not widely understood, and many programs for development soon bog down or limp along in an uneasy direction, resulting in feelings of frustration, anxiety, or guilt rather than growth. I hope to identify some of the directions that an individual's change, vis-à-vis growth and improvement, might take and to delineate some of the forces and conditions, which if understood would facilitate these change goals, since certain pitfalls and stumbling blocks might be avoided or minimized if they can be recognized early.

The most basic organization to shape the direction of individual behavior is the family. Within its confines the individual acquires tools that will direct his future change efforts. If the family is limited in its ability to start in motion the individual processes of growth, then all subsequent organizations that inherit these scantily prepared family members can, possibly, be restricted or handicapped in providing for growth experiences. Thus the family comes in for some attention in this book. The assumption is made that the family system is the system over which most people have most immediate control. It is the place where change can most quickly be implemented with the greatest payoff for all persons involved. Perhaps the family should be the basic laboratory where change methods and strategies are first tried out in order that some skill and competency may be developed for use in the wider society.

Change is also becoming an increasing arena of professional activity. Traditionally there have been certain helping professions whose major area of focus has been change or the solution of problems. Such has usually been the case with ministers, social workers, counselors, therapists, and with many doctors, lawyers, nurses, and teachers. In the past two decades, newer professionals have emerged; such persons have been variously called change agents, consultants, applied behavioral scientists, facilitators, trainers, and organization development specialists. This new breed of professional has as its world the diagnosis of human systems — sometimes from the intrapersonal to the group and then to the larger system. These professionals aim to help that system change in the desired direction on the basis of a carefully considered diagnosis of it.

This is a new profession — challenging, exciting, frustrating, rewarding, sometimes producing anxiety and depression because of the slowness of change or the lack of results. This volume also attempts to help the new professional understand his world and to provide him with some of the tools of the new trade — concepts, insights, diagnostic orientations, and change strategies. The change agent also needs to understand what is going on within the individual as he thinks about his own development process so that there can be a blending of individual and organizational goals for improvement.

This book tries to identify some of the major current values, methods, and theories that underline the process of change. Individual and organizational health in a democratic society seem to push for conditions of more freedom and personal commitment. As we shape a society that gives increasing education to the masses of people, the types of organizations that will utilize these educated persons will also have to change. It now appears that those organizations that can create conditions of greater communications, shared goal setting and decision making, wider involvement of people in planning and implementation — in short, tapping into the wellsprings of human motivation and commitment — are going to be those organizations that will also change and grow positively.

I hope that this volume will give some clarity to individuals, organizational leaders, and professional change agents as to the direction that human growth, at the individual and organizational level, might take — emphasizing that change can be a product that is readily available rather than the chance result for a fortunate few.

This book is written for the following persons:

1. *Persons interested in their own change and growth.* Section 1 is primarily for the person who would like some insight about directions for personal development. This section deals with issues about one's own basic values and orientations as he plans to build more effective relationships with others. Personal growth is always interpersonally oriented in this book, following an assumption that for almost all people one's life and its improvement are inexorably connected with significant others.

2. *Managers of systems.* Most people are managers in a general sense. Anyone trying to achieve goals through the efforts of other people is a manager. Thus parents, teachers, and ministers are managers, as well as people who carry the title of manager, superintendent, director, administrator, supervisor, president, chairman, or foreman. The manager must be concerned about results, goals, or consequences. When results begin to vary in an undesirable direction, the manager should act. Basic to this volume is the notion that almost every system is a human organization and that the mobilizing and releasing of human effort is a critical part of the manager's job. Sections 1 and 2 describe some of the elements that are important to establish in a truly viable human system where human effort is stimulated rather than restricted. The effective manager builds those organization conditions that allow the individual to grow personally while he is working toward the goals of the organization.

3. *Professional consultants and change agents.* Section 3 of the book is directed toward that growing number of professionals whose career goals are to help individuals and organizations to change in desired directions. Such persons will find sections 1 and 2 helpful as a framework for looking at organizational conditions they may wish to develop, in a sense identifying certain change goals. Section 3 spells out in more detail some of the specifics in the strategy, theory, and method of planned change.

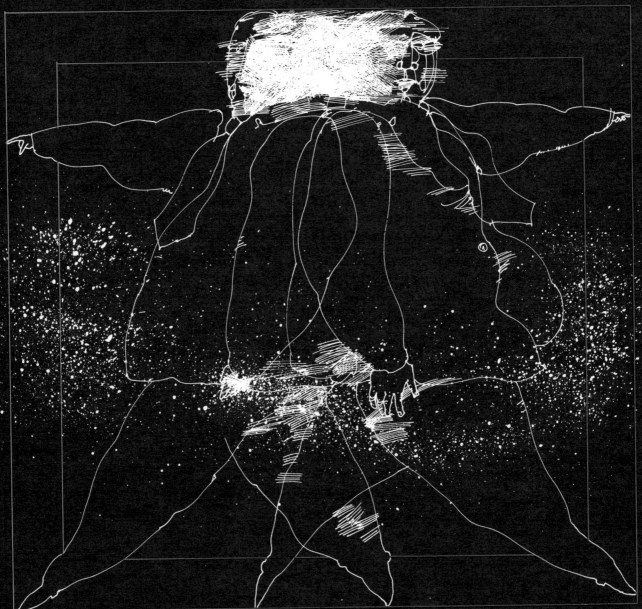

1

Change Directions: The Personal Challenge

This section begins with two articles that represent something of an ideal or goal for personal change. Authentic behavior identifies a goal between people of the type of relationship built on honesty, concern, mutual confidence, and sharing with each other the basic feelings and ideas each has. In this relationship one does not have to put on a front, hide, pretend, or feel guilty or hypocritical.

Basic to an authentic relationship is the personal condition of congruence. For each person congruence means behaving in such a way that there is a harmonious matching of one's observable behavior and his internal life of feelings, values, and goals. In this framework one's actions are congruent or consistent with the kind of person one is inside.

If we are to build a social world in our families, schools, churches, businesses, and communities where people can maximize their own potential and experience growth and deep personal satisfaction, then there are elements that appear to be necessary. Certain of these elements are discussed in the chapters on trust, communications, interdependence, acceptance, and feedback. The chapter on group behavior tries to show those conditions that facilitate the development of people in the group setting.

One important type of change is adjustment. When people cannot accommodate each other's differences through an adjustment process, disruption and conflict occur instead of positive change. The process of adjustment is examined in a marital setting.

Finally there is the problem of motivation. How are people motivated, and what stimulates someone to engage in a change or improvement process? This issue is discussed in the last chapter in this section.

Have you ever found yourself in the following kinds of situations?

1. At a party a person tells an anti-Black story. You resent the story but do not say anything and then feel somewhat ashamed of your own cowardice.

2. You hear a moving talk at a church, civic, or club meeting. After the meeting you want to express your feelings to the speaker, but shyness or something keeps you quiet.

3. There is a moment when you look at your mother, father, spouse, or friend and a wave of deep love and appreciation sweeps over you, but for some reason you say nothing and the moment passes.

4. In a meeting two people engage in a quarrel that is not related to the agenda of the meeting and a great deal of time is wasted. Later the chairman asks how the members felt about the meeting and if anything could be done to improve future meetings. You sit silent.

If you identify with any of the above situations, you are fairly normal. Most of us find it difficult to express our true feelings, especially when we are not sure how people will respond. Currently there is a movement on the part of applied behavioral scientists to reexamine and encourage the building of "authentic" relations, those kinds of relationships between friends, family, church members, co-workers, where people have enough deep concern for each other that they do not always try to hide their true feelings from each other. It is difficult to know exactly how to represent our true selves in particular situations, especially where sensitive areas are involved. Consider the following incidents.

Jeff Hudson was back on campus for his second year. His most recent roommate, Dick Harmon, was a tall, friendly, hard-working young man from a small rural town. It was during the hot, steamy Indian summer that they began their year's relationship. After a busy day in class the two roommates returned to their quarters. Harmon wearily kicked off his shoes, peeled off his socks, and with obvious relief began to systematically clean out the accumulation of dirt and grime between each toe with his forefinger. Jeff watched with a kind of horrified fascination, but he could not bring himself to say anything.

Thereafter Jeff watched this daily ritual with increasing disgust. He began to gripe at Dick constantly, and their relationship disintegrated badly. Dick Harmon was dismayed, for he felt something was wrong, but he couldn't understand what he might be doing to upset his roommate.

Finally, Jeff had reached his limit. One evening as he watched the finger go through Dick's toes, he blurted out harshly, "Dick, I can't stand to watch you do that disgusting thing of cleaning between your toes." Harmon looked up and quietly said, "I'm sorry, Jeff. I didn't know it bothered you. Why didn't you tell me?"

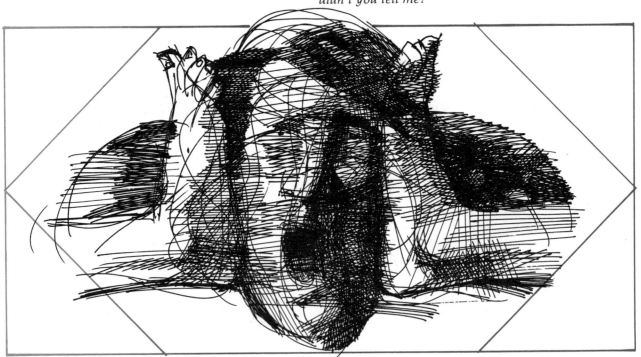

The Dixons were having a husband and wife chat. Mrs. Dixon was confiding in her husband that she was about at her limit in her relationship with their neighbor, an energetic widow — Mrs. Wilson.

"The problem," said Mrs. Dixon, "is that whenever we get together Thelma Wilson always dominates the conversation and the essence of every visit is to listen to her complain about how bad everything is. She is always upset over something or somebody. I sit and listen to her complain about the city government, the poor postal service, the neighbor's dog, the unfriendly neighbor on the other side of her, the ill-mannered Peterson kids, etc., etc. I get so exasperated with her I don't know what to do."

Mr. Dixon listened quietly. He knew, as did his wife, that Thelma Wilson was also a very good neighbor in many ways. She was generous and willing to help others in need, an active church member. He asked his wife, "What do the other women in the neighborhood do with Thelma?"

"We have talked about it," said Mrs. Dixon, "and most of the other girls have handled it by avoiding her as much as possible. They don't feel very good about that, but what else can they do?"

Why didn't Jeff speak out earlier? Why don't the neighbors share their feelings with Thelma Wilson? It isn't easy to tell someone about our feelings concerning their personal habits or behaviors. We are afraid we might offend them or hurt their feelings or they might get angry and attack us, so we keep quiet. Commonly, we might also try to avoid the person and as a result a break does occur in the relationship.

Should we speak out whenever anything a person does bothers us? Obviously not, for if a person's behavior bothers us it is *our* problem. We first need to see if we can expand our margin of tolerance and acceptance so we can accept that person for what he is rather than make him always change so we feel better. However, if the person's behavior violates an important value of ours, or if we find for some reason we cannot expand our margin of acceptance adequately,

Some people find it difficult to let others know if they are hurt, angry, upset, or even if they disagree.

then we should go to the person and talk with him about our feelings of concern. The spirit of the encounter should be one of wanting to improve our relationship, based on a genuine concern for the other person.

Some people find it difficult to let others know if they are hurt, angry, upset, or even if they disagree. They keep those feelings hidden so that they neither resolve them by means of self-understanding and self-dialogue, nor can they discuss them with others in a way that will be helpful rather than hurtful. Still others find it difficult to share their feelings of love, concern, joy, empathy, or appreciation. They keep these feelings locked inside themselves where none can bask in the glow of the shared warmth. These positive feelings need not always be openly expressed, but neither should they always be hidden. The following experience shows the happiness that can come from expressed feelings of love.

It was the day before Christmas when Mr. Brown drove into his driveway after a long day's work. He noticed with interest that the driveway and walks that had been covered with ice and snow when he left for work were now completely cleared. To himself he mused, "I wonder who mother got to do that job."

He went into the house and took off his coat and gloves. In the kitchen he met his oldest boy, a lanky youth of thirteen. "Dad, did you notice the walks were all cleared off?" asked the boy.

"Of course, I couldn't miss that."

The boy then continued. "I didn't have any money to buy you a Christmas present so I cleaned the walks to show you that I love you and appreciate you." And then to the father's deep delight and surprise, his son walked over, put his arms around his father and hugged him tightly in an awkward embrace. The father hugged back, grateful for a gift he would never forget.

Why are we afraid, embarrassed, or reluctant to share our warm and positive feelings with others?

The resistance usually comes from what we *imagine* might happen — the others might get embarrassed; they might suspect our motives; they might cry and that would put us in a situation that would be uncomfortable. We might appear awkward, or we might even cry — and that would be even worse. Sometimes we are stopped because we feel there is not enough time, or too many people are around. The person who fears an authentic encounter with another can find many reasons why he should stay behind his mask and not let anyone know his true feelings.

Shakespeare felt that being authentic was the beginning of moral behavior, "To thine own self be true, / And it must follow, as the night the day, / Thou canst not then be false to any man." To be false to oneself is to not let your behavior represent what you really are like inside.

One man put it this way:

I am tired of having two opposing sets of feelings. When I have pretended to be good and people praise me, I often feel guilty and think, "If they really knew me they probably wouldn't like me." On the other hand, when I have done something inadequately or ineptly and people respond negatively, I think, "If they really knew me, they would like me."

This man decided that the best solution was to try as best he could, all the time, to let his behavior represent what he was truly like inside. Then, if people like that, they really like him, for that is the kind of person he honestly is; and if they don't like that behavior, he knows they don't like him, for he will represent his values as best he can.

Sometimes there are things about ourselves we don't like and would like to change. If we want to be authentic, we have to admit our weakness to others and honestly try to engage in actions that will help us eliminate or change our behavior. A person with a sharp tongue that wounds others' feelings should not say, "That's the way I am; and if I am to be authentic, I will just have to tongue-lash people and hurt them." If that person has other values such as

Being an authentic person is a risk.

wanting to be kind and responsive to others, to build people rather than diminish them, he must be honest to those values too; this honesty would lead him to try to eliminate his sharpness of tongue.

Being an authentic person is a risk. Most of us have hidden behind a facade in some areas for so long it would be a real risk to try to be different. It would be a risk for a teen-age girl to go to a teen-age boy who is a fine example in the high school and say, "Greg, I just want you to know I admire you and appreciate the good example you have set for me and the other kids in school." It would be a risk for a man to go to his boss and say, "I have been complaining about some things in the company to my family and others and I think you should know how I feel. I would like to meet with you and tell you my reactions in a way that I hope might help make this a better place to work." It is a risk for a father who has been silent too many years to tell his twenty-year-old son, "I love you, son. You are the most important thing in the world to me." Just as it would be a risk for the son to share the same feelings with his father.

Behavior change has its price.

It may be true that nothing is gained or learned without a price. Behavior change has its price — anxiety and the possibility of failure. It is also possible that a change in the direction of being more authentic may have rewards that far exceed the costs.

While congruency as a way of behaving has received wide acceptance, many criticize it as (1) giving way to license, (2) not allowing for change, and (3) not really being practical. If we recognize that congruence is not the only value we hold, perhaps we can respond to a range of feelings stemming from a more complex value system. Simple, impulsive behaviors may not represent the range of feelings induced by a complex set of values; to be truly congruent one must be aware of both his values and the range of his feelings. Neither does congruence mean the maintaining of one's behavioral status quo. Congruence would require that a person who has behaviors he does not like should declare these to others and engage in a process of change. Being congruent may not only represent a value but requires skill in performance, and this skill can perhaps be learned. Since certain social systems may not initially support congruent behaviors, it may mean introducing change into the system before congruence is recognized as a practical way of living with others.

Congruent Behavior

The idea of congruence as defined by Rogers (1961) has generated a share of excited acceptance attended by some disturbing criticism. Rogers defines congruence as "the term we have used to indicate an accurate matching of experiencing and awareness. It may still be further extended to cover a matching of experience, awareness, and communication. Perhaps the simplest example is an infant. If he is experiencing hunger at the physiological and visceral level, then his awareness appears to match his experience, and his communication is also congruent with his experience" (1961:308).

Rogers goes on to point out the disruption that occurs in a relationship where there is noncongruent behavior. If I think a person is angry, yet he denies

---

*Revised. Reprinted by special permission from Journal of Applied Behavioral Science. "Congruence and control," William G. Dyer 14 (1969):161-166.

he is angry, my trust of him is diminished and I become wary of him. On the other hand, if the person admits his anger, which is consistent with my experience of him, then I feel he is an honest, trustworthy person; my confidence increases; and the relationship develops around feelings of trust and openness. Thus, according to Rogers, congruence leads to the following general principle:

The greater the congruence of experience, awareness, and communication on the part of one individual, the more the ensuing relationship will involve: a tendency toward more mutually accurate understanding of the communication; improved psychological adjustment and functioning in both parties; mutual satisfaction in the relationship (1961:311).

Conversely, the greater the communicated incongruence of experience and awareness the more the ensuing relationship will involve: further communication with the same quality; disintegration of accurate understanding, less adequate psychological adjustment and functioning in both parties; and mutual dissatisfaction in the relationship (1961:313).

As I have presented this idea to many individuals and groups — while indicating my own acceptance of the general idea of congruent behavior — three main objections usually arise:

1. "Do you mean that a person should always behave exactly as he feels? If I feel like punching you in the nose, raping your wife, or yelling obscenities at you, should I go ahead?" The issue raised here is this: *Does congruence mean giving in to all impulses immediately?*

2. "I have been taught all my life that I should learn to control my anger or negative feelings. Suppose I don't like someone; if I behave as though I do like them, then I will begin to like them. Suppose I feel unhappy; if I try to act happy, then after a while I will feel happier." The issue here is this: *If I behave congruently all the time, will I ever learn to improve on those behaviors in myself that I do not like?*

3. "That congruence bit sounds good but it

Should a person always behave exactly as he feels?

doesn't work. I told my wife the other night that I was really upset with the sloppy way I found the house every day when I came home from work. She was so mad she didn't speak to me for three days and I had to plead for forgiveness and buy her a present and behave in all kinds of noncongruent ways before we got back on an even keel." The issue here is this: *Congruence does not always seem to result in immediate improvement in relationships. Why not?*

Issue One: Does Congruence Mean License?

Central to the first issue is the question: Is congruence synonymous with license? Does it mean that it is all right for a person to behave in any way so long as it is consistent with his current state of awareness and experience? Congruence in this direct and immediate sense *has* become a major value for some. The hippies, for example, stress the hypocrisy of "society" and the lack of congruence they observe in conventional life. Behaving exactly as one feels — refusing to bathe, not working, taking drugs, freely exchanging sexual favors — is the usually represented symbol of the congruent behavior of the hippie subculture, although those acquainted with the movement contend it stands for much more than these stereotyped symbols.

Congruence as a value (implemented, it becomes a style of behavior), favored by Rogers, seems to stem from a set of other kinds of values represented in our culture, in fact, as a counterreaction to certain values. Eric Berne (1964) has popularized the superficial "games" that characterize many human interactions. The "games people play" are the opposite of congruent behavior, and it is just such phony behavior that has given rise to the notion of congruence as an antidote to the prevailing pattern.

We also seem to be living in an emotionally deprived culture where the emphasis is on rational behavior to the restriction of emotional responses. Argyris (1962) and Gibb (1965), among others, have pointed out the dominance of rationality in the management of many organizations, with the resulting disruptive consequences as emotional behavior interferes with ongoing activities — because many persons prefer neither to recognize nor to deal with emotional behavior. Many of the writers who have pointed to this denial of emotional behavior in organizations have suggested that managers need to learn to recognize, accept, and deal more effectively with human emotions. In this sense they are suggesting more "congruence" — more openness of feelings and emotions, and a greater willingness to deal with these feeling-data openly and honestly. These arguments again are a reaction against those norms that support phoniness, maintenance of a facade, gamesmanship, and denial of feelings in behavior. But if congruency is a counter value, how far does it go? What are the limits, if any?

Congruency as a counter value is based on the fact of certain existing control orientations or value orientations already present in traditional society. While they are usually not explicitly mentioned, for most people there are certain already built-in control features that result in congruency within limits. As mentioned above, the problem for many people is not going "too far" with congruency but dealing with overcontrolled behavior.

The great problem with issue number one stems from an assumption that congruency becomes if not the only value a person lives by at least the major value of import. At this level a searching examination of value systems for individuals and organizations becomes critical. One of the issues that has not been handled well is recognizing the personal value systems of participants. Congruency is suggested as a new value without really examining in any depth the other values people hold, including those values they perhaps should relinquish as no longer useful and those values they should cherish and retain.

When I am asked in a Training Group (T-Group) the question raised in issue one: "Do you mean that you are always going to behave exactly as you feel even if you feel like hitting someone or seducing someone?" I answer the participants in this manner: "Being congruent is not the only value I hold. I also value the rights of others. My personal value system stands for trying to live a helpful life with others, to value a society based on mutual respect and acceptance. If I were to engage in behavior that might be 'congruent' at the moment, I would also violate a great many other values that I deem important. I will not violate those values just to be congruent."

The issue then becomes: How do I deal with my hostile, punishing, or devastating feelings? If I were to act them out directly, I would violate certain other values I hold as important. If I deny these feelings and try to repress them, I am aware that the result may be a number of harmful consequences either toward myself (certain psychosomatic difficulties) or in subtle, hostile reactions toward others that are difficult to handle since they are hidden or guarded and can easily be denied. Thus my definition of congruence would encourage me to *express my feelings without necessarily acting them out.* However, this behavior leads to the problem raised in issue two.

Issue Two: Does Congruence Allow for Change?

Here the issue concerns the matter of change. Congruence in its simplest form would require that each person behave according to his current level of awareness and experience. Sometimes we are not happy with that current level; we would like not to feel the ways we sometimes do. We would like to change our pattern of feeling, experiencing, and expressing.

From time to time I encounter a person who accepts certain things about himself as fixed — as a part of his "personality" that is almost immutable. He explains that he should not really be held responsible for the consequences of his actions since "this is the way I am." This reminds me of the story of the scorpion who asked a frog to carry him across a

Being congruent is not the only value I hold. I also value the rights of others.

14

**Replied the scorpion,
"It's in my nature."**

stream. "No," said the frog, "you'll sting me if I do." "Of course not," replied the scorpion, "for if I do, you will sink and we will both be lost." At that the frog agreed and began to ferry the scorpion across the water. In the middle of the stream the scorpion suddenly jabbed the frog with a fatal sting. With his last breath the frog asked, "Why did you do it?" Replied the scorpion, "It's in my nature."

People are not scorpions (although some act the part), and we have learned that the nature of man is not fixed or unchangeable. A person who says, "I'm just a blunt person; if that hurts you, it's just the way I am," would seem to operate on the scorpion theory of personality. A congruence value would seem to give this type of person the perfect rationale to continue behaviors which are "just the way I am" regardless of their consequences to others.

When a person holds a complex of values, an experience will often elicit a range of feelings. To what feeling should one be congruent? Suppose I have strong hostile feelings toward another person to the extent that I feel like punching him in the nose. At the same time another set of values elicits some feelings of guilt about the hostile feelings; these other values suggest to me that I should be trying to "love my neighbor as myself." In fact, these other values direct me toward a goal of trying to understand and accept others the way they are. I do not want to live my life responding in quick, hostile, punishing ways toward others, even if I currently feel that way. I do not want to adopt the scorpion theory that "this is just the way I am"; therefore I will be congruent, and this makes everything justifiable. Certain values suggest change. While congruency *seems* to be a nonchange orientation, congruency in a more complete sense, in my experience, becomes the real basis for change.

If I feel hostile and punishing toward another person and at the same time have feelings of concern or guilt for feeling this way in light of other values, congruency theory would require that I share *all* of these feelings, not just the hostile ones. If I were truly congruent (and this demands that I be aware of *all* my own values and my range of feeling experience), then I should express the range of feelings toward the person in words such as these: "John, when you try to dominate the meeting, I want to punch you in the nose. You make me feel very hostile and angry. But I don't like to feel that way. I also would like to accept you and work with you. How can I work out these feelings with you?"

Accepting and admitting that we do have certain "bad" feelings does not mean that we want to keep them or that we cannot change. My own experience tells me that, if I can express these feelings that I do not like and want to change, making them open to the person in question results in a lessening of these feelings in me and allows me to respond more to the feelings I have that I like better. Should I go so far as to act as though I like a person, even though I do not like him, in the hope that this will result in liking? In light of the discussion above the answer would be no. I should share with the person both my feelings of dislike and my desire to like and engage in a continual interaction which will allow the liking feelings to be enhanced. This should be the result, if there is any validity to the Homans proposition that liking increases with interaction (Homans, 1961).

There is also the matter of timing. Should I express all of my feelings immediately? Does congruency demand immediacy of expression? A common experience for many is that if they "sleep on it" they will feel different later on. Some theories of personality would suggest that this lapse of time does not eliminate the feelings but allows the feelings to become buried in the unconscious part of ourselves. Others feel that through insight and self-dialogue we can resolve certain inner feelings without expressing them to others. This seems to me to be an interesting area for further research and analysis.

Can a person be congruent if he admits his feelings to himself but does not share them immediately and

I want to punch you in the nose.

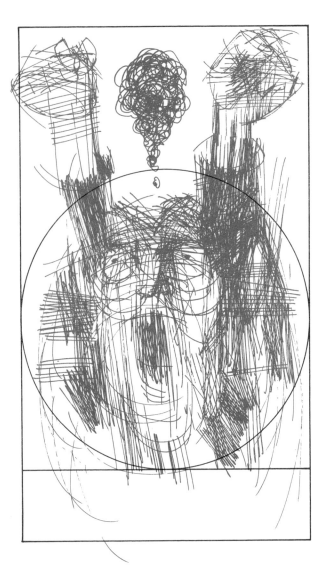

openly with the others involved? Can a person wrestle with his own feelings and the connected sets of values and win a private war within himself, or does congruency demand an open interaction? For me there is no clear answer to these questions. I think I have experienced both conditions. I think I have been able to silently examine my own conflicting feelings and achieve a sense of resolution or congruence, if you will, within myself. On the other hand, I have also experienced (usually in a laboratory setting) the exciting process of letting another person know immediately my feelings about his behavior with a resultant working through of the differences between us. In my experience this has led to a deepening of the relationship as described by Rogers (1961). It may be that the nonopen resolution of feelings toward another does not achieve an enhancement of the relationship, although it may result in a sense of resolution within.

One theory of emotional behavior contends that emotions if not expressed continue to persist and to expand if the "case" of the emotion continues. I am referring to the commonly experienced phenomenon of a person who is continually irritated by another until he finally "can't stand it any longer." At that point there is an explosion of feeling that may actually be stronger than was originally warranted but was allowed to build up by the holding in of the feelings. If this is true of emotional behavior, then it would seem that resolutions of interpersonal conflict would result more easily if dealt with more immediately. It would also seem that if we would be more congruent in the earlier stage of the emotional experience, then our feelings at first would more accurately represent our reaction to the stimulus behavior. When expressed later on, the built-up emotion may not be a good representation of the feeling initially prompted by the behavior of the other. The "waiting game" may allow us to add fuel to the initial feelings as we begin via a selective perception process to see things in subsequent contacts. But then again, it may be that waiting for a time allows us to cool down and that the later emotion does more adequately represent a range of feelings and values if time is allowed for them to converge and interact within us. Again, more thinking and research seem to be needed.

Issue Three: Can Congruence Be Learned?

The nub of issue three seems to be: *How* are we congruent. Some people claim that they have tried congruent behavior and that the result has not been rewarding. Rogers (1961) feels that congruency will result in the enhancement of a relationship. It seems to me that there are differing ways or differing styles that people have of behaving congruently. Congruent behavior for Person A may appear to others as crude, blunt, and punishing, whereas Person B's behavior, also congruently oriented, may be perceived as open, helpful, and trustworthy. Is there not some element of skill in behavior? Is it possible in expressing our feelings toward others to learn ways that communicate better and result in reactions from others more in line with our intentions toward them? It appears to me that one of the reasons for a human relations laboratory is not only to help participants examine a new value like congruency and to see how it fits into their value structure but also to help them develop some behavior skill in implementing this new value.

In discussing feedback, Argyris (1962) points out what I have found to be an important factor in giving helpful feedback: namely, that we remain descriptive and nonevaluative. If this is true, we might then teach people to give nonevaluative feedback. This same condition may be true for all attempts at congruent behavior; that is, learning the skill of expressing our feelings in descriptive, nonevaluative terms. The process stemming from an interaction context may follow a formula expressed like this: "When you did this (describe the action), it made me feel this way (describe as accurately as possible the inner state you now experience)."

Many people worry about congruent behavior.

"How can I present my feelings tactfully so I shall not hurt anyone?" "If I think through what I am going to say and choose my words carefully, then perhaps I shall not get into difficulty." This careful planning and choosing often results in a response that sounds guarded, cautious, rehearsed, and anything but authentic, congruent communication. The descriptive formula may be at least one method of allowing for more immediate, spontaneous congruency.

It should also be recognized that human interaction takes place in a social structure and that despite the skill of the one being congruent social norms and expectations may mediate against a positive response. Each of us interacts with others within the context of a social system where certain norms operate and where each person has a defined position or status and a role definition. The operation of the system expects certain consistent role performances. Some persons in subordinate role positions have reported going back home from a human relations laboratory and trying out new congruent behaviors with disconcerting results. The superiors continue to expect the old subservient behavior of a subordinate. These new congruent behaviors are totally unexpected and are perceived as threatening, and are thus responded to negatively. There is little system support for the new congruent behaviors, and in a short time the person reluctantly abandons the new congruency for the old, more rewarded role behaviors.

Goffman (1959), an astute observer of the interaction scene, describes the social order that exists when people perform as expected:

Ordinarily the definitions of the situation projected by the several different participants are sufficiently attuned to one another so that open contradiction will not occur. I do not mean that there will be the kind of consensus that arises when each individual present candidly expresses what he really feels and honestly agrees with the expressed feelings of the others present. This kind of harmony is an optimistic idea and in any case not necessary for the smooth working of society. Rather, each participant is expected to suppress his immediate heartfelt feelings, conveying a view of the situation which he feels the others will be able to find at least temporarily acceptable. The maintenance of this surface of agreement, this veneer of consensus, is facilitated by each participant concealing his own wants behind statements which assert values to which everyone present feels obliged to give lip service. Further, there is usually a kind of division of definitional labor. Each participant is allowed to establish the tentative official ruling regarding matters which are vital to him, but not immediately important to others, e.g., the rationalizations and justifications by which he accounts for his past activity. In exchange for this courtesy he remains silent or non-committal on matters important to others but not immediately important to him. We have then a kind of interactional modus vivendi. Together the participants contribute to a single overall definition of the situation which involves not so much a real agreement as to what exists but rather a real agreement as to whose claims concerning what issues will be temporarily honored. Real agreement will also exist concerning the desirability of avoiding an open conflict of definitions of the situation. I will refer to this level of agreement as a "working consensus" (1959:9).

Goffman further claims there is a certain "morality" in behaving consistently with one's defined roles:

In stressing the fact that the initial definition of the situation projected by an individual tends to provide a plan for the co-operative activity that follows — in stressing this action point of view — we must not overlook the crucial fact that any projected definition of the situation also has a distinctive moral character. It is this moral character of projections that will chiefly concern us in this report. Society is organized on the principle that any individual who possesses certain social characteristics has a moral right to

There is a certain "morality" in behaving consistently with one's defined roles.

expect that others will value and treat him in an appropriate way. Connected with this principle is a second, namely, that an individual who implicitly or explicitly signifies that he has certain social characteristics ought in fact to be what he claims he is. In consequence, when an individual projects a definition of the situation and thereby makes an implicit or explicit claim to be a person of a particular kind, he automatically exerts a moral demand upon the others, obliging them to value and treat him in the manner that persons of his kind have a right to expect. He also implicitly foregoes all claims to be things he does not appear to be and hence foregoes the treatment that would be appropriate for such individuals. The others find, then, that the individual has informed them as to what is and as to what they ought to see as the "is" (1959:11-13).

Here, then, is a real dilemma for the person who is suddenly confronted with a new value of congruency. This new value may be very appealing, and he may want to adopt it. However, those persons who surround him in his home, work, church, or community setting are not oriented toward this new value; they may expect him to perform as he has done in the past, and rewards will be contingent on a continuation of expected behaviors.

Thus the young husband who goes home and suddenly begins to behave congruently may be seriously violating a whole set of interaction expectations developed with his wife over a long period of time. It would be surprising if she began to respond positively from the first. What is necessary is the changing of the whole nature of the social system. The couple needs to develop together a whole new set of norms, roles, and expectations. The congruency theory would argue that the best way to begin this change is for the husband to begin the new behaviors and then work through the consequences with his wife. Other models of change would suggest that the change agent (the husband, in this case) should not impose change, but that change procedures be a collaborative effort agreed upon by both. It is not uncommon for a husband (or wife) who has attended a laboratory to try to get the spouse to attend also so that together they can begin a new pattern of behavior based on a common frame of reference. Many organizations use a laboratory experience for the same purpose: they send teams of managers to laboratories so that they can adopt new behaviors for the system based on a common new experience.

Summary

In this discussion I have been trying to look at some of the problems which a person who adopts a new value of congruency may expect to encounter. If these conditions are recognized, congruent behavior may be successful.

1. Congruency as a value is not the only value a person holds. To be congruent he must still behave consistently with old values or begin the process of reevaluation of his value system and begin to abandon or modify old values.

2. If one's values are in contradiction, the congruency stance is one effective method of beginning the process of personal value change. That is, one can begin to verbalize the ambivalence one feels and involve others in the process of examining the problems that result in the relationship.

3. Congruency does not mean that people cannot change. Certain values may support behaviors that we like better than others, even if we do not feel or behave in the desired way now. By expressing our current state of feelings and also our desires for improvement, we enter into a process that would seem to help us move toward the desired behavior goals.

4. Congruent behavior may take more skill than one now possesses. One possibility is that learning to be congruent via a descriptive rather than an evaluative process may result in the type of response more consistent with the end result wished for in the relationship.

5. There are many conditions in the social systems within which interaction takes place which may be resistant to new, congruent behaviors. These structured role definitions and expectations may need to be altered through a change process before congruency as a reciprocal process can be engaged in by all.

References

Argyris, Chris
1962   Interpersonal Competence and Organizational Effectiveness. Homewood, Illinois: Irwin-Dorsey Press.

Berne, Eric
1964   Games People Play. New York: Grove Press.

Gibb, Jack R.
1965   "Fear and facade," in R. Farson, Science and Human Affairs. Palo Alto, California: Science and Behavior Books, Inc.

Goffman, Erving
1959   The Presentation of Self in Everyday Life. Garden City, New York: Doubleday.

Homans, George
1961   Social Behavior, Its Elementary Forms. New York: Harcourt, Brace & World.

Rogers, Carl
1961   On Becoming a Person. Boston: Houghton Mifflin.

A mother was talking with a high school principal: "I just can't seem to do anything with Tom anymore, Mr. Bickmore. We used to talk together a lot but now he seems defiant and rebellious, and we seem to be fighting all the time. I know that since he has been in high school he has been more tense and nervous than before. He hides things from me, won't tell me where he's going, or what he's doing. I'm afraid that he might get into some kind of trouble, and I know he's not doing well in school. What can I do?"

The principal thought for a while, "Well, Mrs. Scott, it seems that Tom may have some problems that he doesn't feel free to talk about with you. If you could build more of a feeling of trust with him, perhaps he would begin talking with you again. My advice is to work on improving the feelings of confidence and trust you have between the two of you."

The principal may indeed be right. A family needs to be improved and the advice to "work on" the relationship may be good, but the major question is still unanswered: *How do you go about building a trust relationship with another person?* One of the most common clichés used in talking about the basis of effectively working with other people is that you must first "build a good relationship" or stated other ways, "develop rapport," or "establish a good climate," or "gain their confidence." Unfortunately most discussions stop at this point as though the subject were covered having stated the principle. Each person is left to his own devices as to what should be done in establishing the critical base of the whole subsequent relationship.

Factors in Trust

When a person says of another, "I don't trust him," what is usually implied? A critical dimension is honesty. Trust here is a sense of confidence that another person's word is an accurate representation of what he will do. It is hard to "trust" a person who says one thing yet behaves in another way. Under-

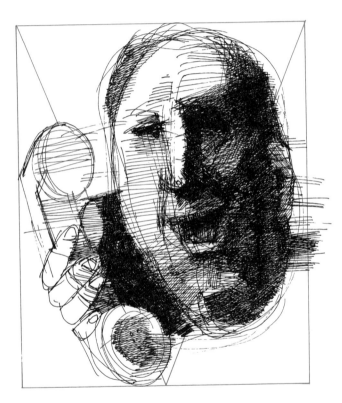

lying all trust relationships is the willingness to put something of ourselves in the care of another. We do not want to put our secrets or confidences in a person who will not keep them. We do not want to make decisions with people that involve something of our time, energy, and resources, if we are not sure that the person will actually follow through on an agreed decision. Whether we call it honesty or integrity, basic to a relationship of trust is the sense that one can count on another person to do what he represents himself to do.

Members of families are often not aware of all the things they do that destroy trust.

"Dad, will you come and play ball with me." "Sure, son, just as soon as I finish this task." One hour later. "Dad, aren't you going to come and play ball like you said?" "I'm sorry, son, but I got busy doing something else; we'll play ball another time."

Dad: "Ann, I hear that you've got a new boy-friend — only he doesn't know about it yet (teasing). I think I'll call him up and tell him to watch out for you."

Ann (to her mother): "Mother, how could you tell Dad when I specifically asked you not to say anything to anybody."

Mother: "Oh, it doesn't matter if your Dad knows. After all, he's only kidding about calling him up."

A common device used by many parents is to promise things to children in the hopes that the child will forget about the request in the passing of time, and by making the promise it placates the child and keeps him from "bothering" the parent. Often there is no intention on the part of the parent that the promise will be kept. Then when the child does not mention the matter again, there is an assumption made that the child has forgotten the matter and that the strategy worked. Parents might well operate from the other assumption: that children do not really forget anything and that any violation of one's word will contribute to a decrease in the trust relationship.

Caring

Fundamental to a trust relationship is the feeling one person has that the other person "cares" for him. Caring here is equated with concern for or interest in the other person. It is not the same as liking or affection. It is possible to have feelings of affection for a person you don't basically trust, and as a result you hold back some things about yourself from that person.

The feeling of being cared for is a very subtle quality.

Two high school girls went on a double date to a school dance. After the dance, the two couples went to a local cafe for something to eat. They ate and talked and forgot about the time. About 1:30 the mother of one of the girls suddenly appeared at their booth. She was still in her nightgown with a coat thrown over her shoulders. Looking directly at her daughter, she said, "I told you that if you were not home by 1:00 that I was coming after you. Come with me, young lady." And with that she marched her daughter out of the cafe and home.

The next day the two girls met and talked. The one girl was terribly mortified about her mother's actions. But the other girl's reactions were interesting. She said, "I wish my mother cared enough about me to come and get me. She doesn't care what I do or when I come home."

Which of these two mothers was beginning to build or destroy a trust relationship? The one girl whose mother came after her may have felt that her mother did not trust her, and this lack of feeling trusted may erode the relationship. On the other hand, the other girl's mother may have been trying to display trust in her daughter, but the daughter interpreted this as a lack of caring. There is a fine interplay between these two qualities — caring and placing trust in others. People should be shown that others are concerned about the consequences of their actions and are willing to invest something of themselves in terms of time, intimacy, and personal warmth to show that concern. A common phrase used to indicate that we have no concern for another person is, "I couldn't care less." If a person feels that others in the family are not concerned enough about him to invest any of their own personal resources in his behalf, it would be predicted that trust will be low. The investment of personal resources really means giving up something of real value on behalf of the other person. Many parents with money give money to their children but reserve their more precious resources such as time, warmth, and intimacy, still expecting their children to have this close, trusting relationship. Parents should assume that children are able to perceive the giving of something that is of personal worth in contrast to the giving of something that does not represent a real investment of self.

Trusting

If trust is to be built between people, then a mutuality of confidence must be exchanged. It is virtually impossible to build a trust relationship if one party in the relationship says in effect, "I want you to trust me and to have a trust relationship, but I don't really trust you to keep your word, to show judgment, or to be responsible. I am trustworthy, but you are not."

Often this is what parents communicate to children when they "check up" on their children. Consider the following:

Mother: "Susan, I want you in by 1:00 p.m. after your date tonight. Is that agreed?"

Susan: "All right, Mother, I'll be in then."

Mother: "Just to make sure that you're in, I'm going to set my alarm for 1:00. If you're in by then, just snap the alarm off; but if you're not, then I am going to get up and then we will just have to see what happens."

This mother is saying in effect, "Daughter, you say you will be on time, but I don't really trust you to be honest or responsible; so I am going to check up just to make sure." Some mothers would say that the only reason they would set the alarm is that they are concerned, and checking up is just showing concern. Here again is that sensitive balance between showing concern and showing confidence or trusting another person. It seems that in some families there is the assumption that a person is untrustworthy until he proves he can be trusted. A trust relationship seems to develop easier from the opposite premise; namely, that a person is considered trustworthy until proven otherwise. At least this is consistent with our notions of guilt or innocence.

Suppose in the above situation the daughter and her date had a flat tire or were detained for some legitimate reason. The setting of the alarm clock will not change that. However, it might alert the mother to mobilize some help, and this is usually given as the reason for a "check-up" system. Usually it results that the mother must allow the daughter to cope with the situation in her own way since the mother is out of the situation.

Also suppose the daughter is untrustworthy; evidence from research in other systems points out that a checking-up system is no real deterrent to an untrustworthy person. In fact, they try to "beat" the checking-up system. An untrustworthy daughter could come in, snap off the alarm, and then sneak back out. The mother would then have to think up another system to check up on her daughter, and the daughter would probably try to beat the new system. Thus there would be a constant strategy-counterstrategy game going on between mother and daughter, which is the exact opposite of a trust relationship.

It is often extremely difficult for parents to trust their children to make wise decisions when the decision the child makes is different from the parent's under the same circumstances. Does trusting another person, particularly a child, mean that he is allowed to do what he wants to do? Trusting at that point is entwined closely with freedom. How much freedom and autonomy can we entrust to a child? Parents are constantly fearful that their children will make

A checking-up system is no real deterrent to an untrustworthy person.

mistakes that will have long-range, painful consequences; and as a result they are afraid to allow too much freedom to their children. But maturity and judgment come as a child learns to make decisions and to profit from his own experiences. It is not good child training when the parent makes all the choices, eliminating the child's right to experiment and learn. He needs to learn to use freedom wisely and to become trustworthy so that when he becomes an adult he is able to then make choices and decisions on his own.

It is possible for a parent to have the type of relationship with a child where there is a real confidence between them, a sense of trust and concern, a mutuality of sharing, and an openness of communication. Then the child seeks the opinions and experiences of the parents, and matters can be discussed openly and freely. Out of that free exchange, the child makes his own decisions with a degree of confidence, knowing he has gathered adequate data and that his decisions will be respected by his parents.

Openness

An important part of building trust is developing a system of openness in communication. It is difficult to trust another person if we feel he will not tell us everything that is important to know about situations of mutual concern. Openness has at least two dimensions: *sharing*— letting others know our personal thoughts, ideas, opinions, feelings, experiences, and reactions; and *leveling*— being honest and candid in letting others know how we feel about them and their behavior.

Some families have very little sharing; that is, people do not share their daily experiences, troubles, concerns, or joys with each other. Parents often want their children to share with them but do very little sharing in return. A common table conversation goes something like this:

Dad: "Well, Bob, how was school today?"
Bob: "O.K., I guess."

> Parents often want their children to share with them but do very little sharing in return.

Dad: "Tell me what happened today, anything interesting?"

Bob: "Nah, just the same old stuff."

Dad to mother: "It's like pumping water out of a dry well trying to get any information out of that boy."

What the father should realize is that he has probably shared very little of his day with anyone, in fact, the same conversation probably took place between mother and dad when he came home and she wanted to find out what he was doing during the day. Just as caring begets caring, and trusting elicits trusting, so does sharing bring forth more sharing. If one family member can begin to share more of himself with others, it will begin to open the way for others to share. Family members then begin to feel that other family members trust them enough to share things of real concern and importance with them. Most children can recall times when they have come upon their parents discussing something that is abruptly halted as soon as the child comes into the room. This leads to a great deal of curiosity and the temptation to eavesdrop to find out what they weren't supposed to hear. Perhaps there are some very sensitive matters that might not be appropriate for children at some ages, but if the children feel that parents are constantly filtering or screening out the conversation, then feelings that the parents do not trust the children begin to develop. Children then learn to be careful of what they say in return, and a low sharing relationship begins to develop.

Leveling is a specific form of sharing, namely letting the other person know how we feel about his behavior.

Wife to husband who has just come home from work and has completely ignored her and is sitting in the front room reading the paper: "John, when you come home and don't even come in and spend any time with me, it makes me feel very angry and resentful toward you, and I feel like punishing you back in some way."

30

Here the wife is letting the husband know *what he has done* by describing his behavior and also *how it makes her feel* by describing her inner state of feeling. She is leveling with her husband, being very honest about her negative feelings, but in a non-judgmental way. Evaluative, judgmental leveling would go something like this: "John, you never pay any attention to me at all. You are only concerned about yourself and what you want to do. You're more interested in the paper than you are in me. I wish you would quit being so inconsiderate and selfish and think of someone else just once." John is being evaluated negatively as being selfish, inconsiderate, never paying attention to his wife, and so on. Obviously, John is going to defend himself against these judgments in some way, and the leveling attempt by his wife may lead to greater disruption or perhaps a reluctant and uneasy modification of John's behavior, just to placate his wife.

Leveling comes out of the other dimensions of the trusting relationship — out of a sense of concern for

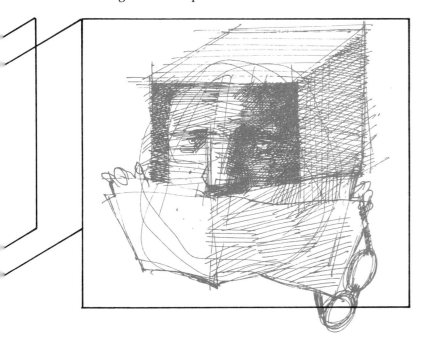

another person we let him know how we feel about his behavior. This is vital; for, if the person feels that leveling is motivated by revenge or punishment rather than concern and acceptance, it is likely to lead to a disruption of the relationship rather than enhancing the trust.

Family status often affects leveling. Father and mother with the highest status often are quite free to level with their children, but don't allow children to give them the same honest reactions. At its best, leveling is a two-way communication process. Parents need to know how their children respond to their behavior just as well as the children need to know the parents' reactions to them. Leveling also involves both positive and negative reactions. It is important for family members to know when they are liked and appreciated, in addition to finding out those things they do that elicit negative responses.

Trust is enhanced in the family if each family member can count on a high degree of openness from all other family members. Family members can be "trusted" to let others know what they are thinking — to share deeply with the family — and each family member can trust others to let him know, in a spirit of helpfulness, when he is engaging in behaviors that create problems for others. Members also know when they are liked and appreciated — all of which contribute to a trusting relationship. It is difficult to trust a person when you don't know where you stand with him; just as it is difficult to trust a person deeply who will not let you know what's bothering him or what his real concerns are. Openness is therefore an essential part of trust.

Openness is an essential part of trust.

Warning: Communication is a means to an end — not an end in itself. We can use communications to hurt, punish, and offend, or we can use communications to bind together, increasing love and joy. The great skill is *not* to get people to communicate more, but to communicate wisely and effectively. Too many families already communicate too many of the wrong things, and to encourage them to communicate more of the same would compound the disaster. Other families suffer from communication shortage — too many things remain unsaid and are not discussed.

Unintended Communications

Very simply, communication is the process whereby one person by the use of symbols (words, actions, gestures, etc.) gets others to understand how he thinks and feels. But sometimes we send out signals, unintentionally, that let people know how we feel when we might have preferred to have kept those feelings hidden.

One of the problems in most families is that in certain areas the communication system is too good; that is, more is communicated than is really intended. We marvel at the sensitivity of the gleaming fingers of the radio antenna and their ability to pluck sound waves from the air. But marvelous, too, is the sensitivity of a little child whose receptors are able to pick up all kinds of messages. One study of little babies found that if a baby were fed orange juice by a nurse who did not like orange juice that in a short time the baby would not drink orange juice. However, if the nurse liked orange juice, so did the baby. Somehow, the nurse was able to communicate to the child her distaste for orange juice via tenseness, grimacing, or shuddering at the sight of the baby drinking the "nasty stuff."

If babies are sensitive enough to pick up from the nurse how she feels about orange juice through her

---

[*]Revised. Reprinted by special permission from The Improvement Era, "Improving family communications," William G. Dyer (April 1963).

subtle body actions, what messages are children receiving from parents in the following make-believe incidents?

Father talking to mother in the car on the way home from a Parent-Youth meeting: "What a boring meeting that was. I don't know the last time we had a really good speaker. I'd have gained more from staying home and reading a good book."

Father to son, a week later: "What! You don't want to go to the Parent-Youth meeting? I can't understand that. You never see me staying home from those meetings! I think they are important for good family relationships!"

One might guess that the father, unintentionally, has really communicated to his children what his true feelings about such meetings are; namely, that the good meeting (not found very often) is one where there is a speaker who is interesting and entertaining (to father).

Another interpretation of the above case may be

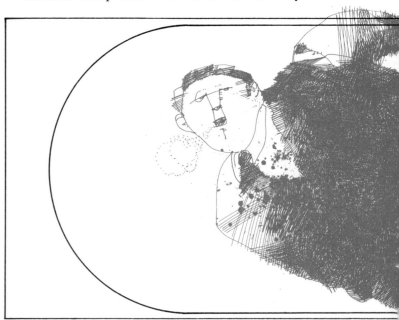

that the father may have both positive and negative feelings about going to Parent-Youth meetings. He may have enjoyed the topic, the general discussion, but disliked the speaker. However, his pattern of communication, developed over a long period of time, is to talk only about the things he dislikes, thus his children may be unaware of his other feelings.

Thus we have the dilemma of unbalanced communications — the father has communicated too much about his negative feelings and too little about his positive feelings.

Father to daughter: "I think you ought to read more of the good magazines we get each week instead of the trashy fan magazines you read all the time. After all, we spend good money for those publications."

Father to mother the next day: "Any mail today? Oh, just the news magazine. We haven't had any important mail for a long time."

Children pick up all of the communicative symbols

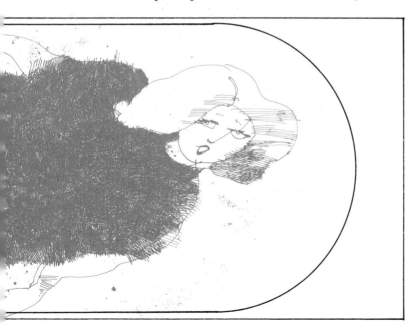

the parents give — not just the words spoken directly to them. In the above illustration, the father's intentions in his direct communications with his daughter are to encourage her to read good publications more, but his unintended communications tell her that he really thinks such material is not too important, as compared with other matters. He is also saying that he is concerned more about wasting money than he is about the reading.

Son to father: "Dad, will you come and help me fix my wagon?" Father: "Just a minute, son, I'm busy right now reading the evening paper." Later. Father: "Son, come and eat; it's time for dinner." Son: "Just a minute, Dad, I'm fixing my wagon." Father: "Not in 'just a minute', when I call you I want you to come right now."

What is the father unintentionally communicating to his son? The son perhaps "hears" that there are two standards — one for him and another for the father, or he hears that his father's newspaper is more important than helping him with his problems. If we were to ask the father, "What is more important, your newspaper or your son's problems?" he would undoubtedly insist that his son is more important. But in a number of subtle ways he has communicated to his son that the newspaper, or the television program, or the golf game, etc., really come first in actual practice.

The above cases indicate that unintentionally we communicate to the other person our likes, dislikes, preferences, and disgusts. It would appear that at least one important basis of "good" communications is not to learn how to say the words better, but to examine ourselves and begin to alter those attitudes, feelings, and reactions that we would not like to see fostered in our children.

Blocked Communications

One of the strange paradoxes of human interactions is that at the same time people are unintentionally communicating things about themselves to others,

they are also being very careful to avoid, hide, camou-
flage, or ignore other things about themselves and
others, and in such areas there is little communication — intentional or unintentional.

*Marriage Counselor: "Mrs. Gray, what seems to
be the biggest problem you have with your husband?"
Mrs. Gray: "Since we have been married my husband is thoughtless and neglectful. He no longer
praises me or tells me he loves me. He forgets birth-
days and anniversaries. He doesn't perform the
courtesies and niceties that I would enjoy so much."
Counselor: "Have you ever told your husband how
you feel?" Mrs. Gray: "I should say not. If he isn't
understanding enough to sense how I feel, I'm certainly not going to say anything. Besides, if I did,
he would just get sore and tell me off."*

This case illustrates one of the great human problems. In all kinds of situations people have their
feelings hurt by others, they are disappointed, upset,
irritated, but they take great pains to hide these feelings from those who would benefit from knowing
how they really feel. One would guess that in the
case above the wife gives off certain signals, inten-
tionally or unintentionally, that let her husband
know that she is upset. It is also quite possible that
even though he knows she is upset he doesn't know
what he has done to cause this. It is almost impossible
for a person to improve unless he knows what he has
done that is wrong.

Why don't people communicate more freely with
each other? Why don't children tell their parents
about the problems they are having? Why doesn't
Mrs. Gray tell her husband?

Perhaps the parents have given off unintentional
signals that make the child feel his problems are
unimportant and will not be listened to. But more
often the imagined consequences of telling another
how we feel are too terrifying, and silence seems to
be the safer course.

*Father to daughter: "No, you cannot take the car
to pick up your girl friend and go to your class party.*

You are still too young to drive at night. You can either walk or I'll drive you over; and, if your teacher can't bring you home, you call and I'll come and get you. Also, since it's a school night, be sure and be home by 10:30."

Mary: "Oh, all right, Father." (To herself: Why is he so unreasonable. Here I am almost seventeen and I'm the only one of our crowd who can't take the car at night. And it's embarrassing to have to leave the party — the earliest of anyone. He treats me like a baby.)

The outsider looking at this situation might say that both the father and the daughter have some legitimate points in their argument — why don't they talk it over and work out a mutually agreeable solution? Why doesn't Mary tell her father how she feels? Experience may have taught her that her father will not consider her point of view, or that if she speaks up her father gets angry at her for being impertinent. She may be afraid that she might cry or get too upset, or it could be she has never talked over important things with her father and just doesn't know how. Perhaps she thinks her father will punish her by taking away all of her car privileges — or even worse, give her the "cold, silent treatment" accompanied with that hurt "how-could-you-do-this-to-me" look.

And the father — why doesn't he talk this over with his daughter instead of just telling her — surely he can see (from the silent signals) that she is upset. It could be that he thinks that children should obey parents — not talk back. After all, that's how he was raised by his father. Or perhaps he fears a tearful scene, and to give the order and retreat behind the newspaper is just easier, and less time consuming.

So the father and daughter do not talk because each has roadblocks in the path of open communications. How can they get rid of these blocks — presuming that they really want to? People and situations are complex and different and there are no simple answers, but there are some guideposts from which we might build a strategy to help meet the situation.

Guidepost 1.

Reexamine Your Assumptions

We all assume things about others that may not be true — but we behave as though they were true. How tragic if the assumptions that we hold and think are true are really false. Mrs. Gray assumes that if she tells her husband how she feels he will "get sore and tell her off." He may have done that once five years ago, and she assumes he is still like that. Mary assumes that if she tries to talk to her father he will get angry and punish her, but maybe he won't. Wouldn't both Mrs. Gray and Mary do better to assume that the husband or father loves them, wants to have a good relationship, and if approached in love and kindness will respond with love and understanding?

Guidepost 2.

Take a Risk

In a sense this is the old adage, "Nothing ventured, nothing gained." When we open the communications channels, we sometimes risk the possibility that the other person may get upset, angry, and may feel hurt or resentful, but we are also risking the possibility that the situation will improve and the end result will be better. Is the reward worth the risk?

Guidepost 3.

Build a Climate of Trust and Understanding

By our actions and expressions let others know that we trust them and accept them. Parents need to let children know that they will accept the child's point of view, will listen to his argument, and will respect his opinion. More than this, the parent needs to say, "I respect you and trust you enough to share my real feelings with you, to confide in you." Sharing begets sharing, openness of communications begets openness from others.

**Each trial is a
learning experience.**

Guidepost 4.

Try — And Learn from the Trying

As we take a risk and make a new trial, we may make mistakes. Our communications may be misunderstood, but each trial is a learning experience — we have learned what not to do. Perhaps next time will be better. If others know we are really trying to do better, this may enhance the climate, lessen the risk, and make the next attempt easier and more successful.

Guidepost 5.

Keep Talking

The easiest thing to do when our communications are misunderstood or produce the wrong result is to lapse into silence, to avoid the issue, or pretend it was never said. Usually we have to clear the communications by adding more communications — in the right kind of climate.

"Don't help me, Mother, I want to do it myself."
This was the comment of a six-year-old to her mother,
who wanted to help her tie her shoes. Almost every
child has this early desire to do things on his own
and be competent enough to achieve or accomplish
something with his own skills, not relying on others
to come in and aid.

"Mother, I can't do it. You've got to help me."
Another comment from the same little girl, who is
now trying to cut out pictures with an awkward
instrument called scissors. In this same child is also
a need to rely on someone, to depend on another
person when she needs assistance.

These two crosscurrents seem to be present in all
of us — the need to be free, independent, and capable
of doing things on our own, and the need to be dependent, to have the right and the luxury of putting
ourselves in the hands of others when our own
resources are insufficient.

Parents and leaders see these apparently conflicting needs in children and other followers; and, depending on their own understanding of themselves
and the people they lead, they respond in ways that
may or may not result in the growth of the child or
the subordinate, and thus enhance the relationship
between the two. It is *from* the authority person that
the child or subordinate person is trying to break free
and demonstrate his own competence, and it is *to* the
authority person one goes when he needs support
and assistance. Central in the performance of any
leader — parent, supervisor, or executive — is the
manner and method he uses to respond to the needs
in others.

Some parents' style of behavior reinforces and
supports the dependency of their children, with the
long-range consequence that the child is incapable of
functioning adequately on his own. For instance,
Jane is a college sophomore. She calls home at least

---

*Revised. Reprinted by special permission from Ensign, "Inter-
dependence: a family and church goal," William G. Dyer (February 1971):35-39.

three times a week to talk with her parents, to get their advice on her courses, purchases she is going to make, activities she is considering. She feels uneasy and insecure when she has to make a decision before talking with her mother and dad. Her parents are openly pleased with Jane, and they tell their friends with pride that Jane is a real home girl who loves her family — not one of those wild types of college students. They are glad Jane relies on their judgment and that she so often calls home for advice. They feel needed and important, and their relationship with their daughter is very satisfying to them.

This example points out some of the elements of a strong dependency-development relationship. The persons in the authority positions (in this case the parents) are using the subordinate person (the daughter) to meet many of their own needs. They would probably be indignant and hurt if it were suggested that they are selfish, for being selfish in the sense that they are concerned about themselves at someone else's expense is not part of their conscious motivation. But in a real sense they are selfish, for they unknowingly have been meeting more of their own needs without considering the long-range well-being of their daughter.

There are times when dependency is legitimate and useful. Occasions will arise in which a person needs help beyond his own resources. All of us must at times depend on others — doctors, teachers, counselors, repairmen, friends, parents — when conditions face us that are beyond our resources to handle effectively alone. Dependency becomes crippling when a person no longer seeks to develop his own resources or to move to a more collaborative stance with persons in authority, but automatically assumes he cannot do anything without the guidance, support, and influence of others.

All human beings start out in life from a position of almost complete dependency on others. The development of the child away from complete dependency is the responsibility of those adults who occupy posi-

All of us must at times depend on others.

tions of authority over him. *How to use authority to help others grow is the major challenge of every parent and every person in a position of authority.*

Too often authority persons become concerned with the wrong goals — parents want children who are only well behaved; teachers want only quiet classrooms or students who will do and say what the teachers want; administrators want subordinates who will obey without question, who are yes-men. One way to achieve these goals is to create dependency in others. Interestingly enough, many dependency-producing leaders never recognize their part in the problem, for they will often exclaim sadly, "What we need is more people who will take initiative and won't just sit around waiting to be told what to do."

In the other behavioral stream is the desire to be free, to "let me do it by myself." Some have postulated, as did the English philosopher Thomas Hobbes, that the basic nature of man is a condition in which every man is at war with everyone else as each tries to hammer out his own ego-centered world. If everyone actually does only what he wants, without taking others into account, we have anarchy.

As parents see this tendency in their children, they often try to stifle, reduce, or change it. Children don't want to share their toys with others, but parents want them to share. Children don't want to eat certain foods, but mother wants them to clean their plates.

There seems to be a subtle (and sometimes not so subtle) struggle going on between the adults, who want to channel or control, and the youngsters, who want to be independent and free to do as they please. It is this basic struggle that underlies counter dependency. Some people get caught up in a resistance pattern to those in authority and expend much time and energy in finding ways to resist the influence of those over them. They can always find a reason why the desires of the authority person can't or shouldn't be carried out, and they proceed to demonstrate this.

Sometimes this negative response is the result of a wrong approach by the authority, be he parent, teacher, boss, or leader. Perhaps the authority initiates directions toward the subordinate in a way that is demeaning and robs the individual of personal dignity. Often no allowance is made for questions or discussion or dialogue — the parent wants his child to obey, "with no back talk." Such an attitude creates in many persons a strong, rebellious reaction.

Some leaders seem deliberately to create situations where the subordinate questions or resists, so that the authority person can "show who is boss" and thus gain a kind of secret delight in dominating another human being.

It should not be assumed, however, that when resistance and reaction occur it is always the fault of the authority person. Often the authority person may be behaving in a very appropriate manner, but the subordinate has been so conditioned to resent and rebel against authority that, no matter how the superior acts, the subordinate always responds negatively. Sometimes this means that in order to achieve a new and more effective level of interaction, both subordinate and authority persons need to reexamine their attitudes and behavior and work out a change.

The type of relationship that is both possible and desirable between authority and subordinates is called *interdependence* — the cooperative or collaborative using of each other's resources. Independence is not used, for it suggests that the subordinate is freed from those in authority and goes his own way. Independence is not the most effective action in today's world, whether it be the family, school, church, business or government organization, community, nation, or world. Of necessity we are an interdependent people. Unfortunately, most people have not learned to be interdependent with others. From writers and researchers in the field of human behavior we have the following actions that can be taken by one in authority and will lead toward greater interdependence.

Love and Concern

Any subordinate person must know that the person in authority over him really cares about him, not just that he does what he is told.

Love for the individual should be unconditional, although we may not love certain of his actions. Too many parents and other authorities present conditional love as the basis of a relationship: "I will love you only on condition that you do what I want, will be dependent on me, and will meet my needs." Such a basis leads to either dependency or rebellion.

Parents need to talk about their feelings of love and concern with their children, church leaders with members, bosses with subordinates. Feelings of the heart need to be shared, no matter how awkward or difficult it may be to do so. And it must be done *now*. Delay only increases the development of the relationship in negative directions.

Feelings of the heart need to be shared.

Trust

Authority persons need to begin to display greater confidence and trust in those under them. Parents need to trust their children to make correct decisions, and they need to give them that opportunity. The fearful authority is afraid others will make mistakes or won't do the job just the way he would do it, so he hovers around, watching, checking up, until he makes them feel like the six-year-old fumbling with her shoelaces.

Trust means allowing — allowing others to perform with a sense of confidence that they are supported by that person over them. Trust means being consistent and trustworthy so the person being directed has confidence in the words and actions of the authority person.

Open Communication

A vital ingredient is the open sharing of information. Communication implies that there is a sender and a listener, and there is understanding between the two. In interdependence, both authorities and subordinates have a chance to send and to listen. It is not a one-way communication system where the authority tells and others are always supposed to listen. In communication we need to share our thinking and our feelings. On almost every subject or issue people have thoughts, ideas, or opinions as well as feelings. If we want true understanding, we must share both kinds of data.

Many parents share little of their own feelings or ideas with their children. Giving directions, orders, and commands is *not* sharing. Sharing comes first, before the decisions are finally made, and is a process of getting thoughts and feelings out in the open so a good decision can be made.

Before decisions are made, the authority person should say, "I want to know what you think and how you feel about the issue at hand. I truly want this information. I will not judge you or punish you for being entirely truthful and candid. If we can both put all our cards on the table, and if we really have concern for each other and trust each other, we can come up with solutions that will be satisfying to all."

Shared Decisions

Interdependence requires that decisions be made in a collaborative way, with all participants understanding each other and coming to a solution they feel good about and are willing to support. Shared decisions are not necessarily fifty-fifty decisions, in the sense that each person will always demand an equal part in everything. Sometimes the father will say, "Son, you have more experience with cars than I do; I trust you to make the decision and I'll support it." At other times the son will respond similarly to the father, and yet at other times each will have to listen to the other and work out a solution both can support and implement.

Joint Action

Interdependence means working together. The carrying out of decisions requires that people work together. In too many families, parents tell their children what to do. The parents pressure, control, or punish until the child does what they demand. Too little work is planned and carried out together, where all experience the delight of a team effort, the accomplishment of things done collaboratively.

Sometimes the work requires effort alone, but it is more satisfying if it can be shared with others.

In our society we see all around us the consequences of young people in rebellion. They are either in revolt against authority or have never learned how to work with authority persons. Training in collaborative problem solving and team effort must be taught in the home. This does not mean parents allowing their children license to do whatever they please, nor does it mean children slavishly carrying out the whims of parents; rather, it is a solid condition of mutual effort based on love, concern, and trust.

A hardcore fact of our society is that most of the activities in which we engage ourselves are within the context of a functioning group. How do these various groups contribute to the ultimate goal we often express to ourselves that we want to produce mature, creative, healthy, happy individuals?

Argyris (1957) of Yale has pointed out that children in our culture start out at an immature state — dependent, subordinate, submissive, conforming, and using only a few surface skills. What we profess to desire in these children is to see them achieve a level of maturity where they are finally independent, creative, have leadership potential, initiate action, and utilize all of their skills. It is Argyris' thesis that the types of groups and organizations into which we funnel our children tend to maintain them at the original level of immaturity.

If we look at many of our schools, social clubs, religious groups, and later on our industrial and business groups, we find that if a person is to get along best in these situations he remains submissive, obedient and conforming, dependent, and is encouraged to use only a few of his skills. However, the individual often realizes he has unused potential and may become frustrated, angry, hostile, withdrawn, rebellious, and a number of other adjectives we use to describe people who are "disturbed." We centralize authority, control, and rewards in these organizations and tend to foster dependency, conformity, and obedience by having people compete with each other for these rewards. In other words, in families, schools, and work groups, when the authority is centralized in the parents, teachers, or bosses — what kind of behavior do we reward? Parents idealize the child that is "so well behaved" — similarly teachers like the child who "does what he is told." Anxiety is created along with possible frustration and hostility when the person is faced with reward or lack of reward. Employers have economic sanction, but parents and teachers have the greater weapon — *affection*. The individual may continue to act in ways we describe as "childish" and "immature," when in fact his total social development has not shown him or allowed him to act in a mature fashion. Let me spell out in more detail some of the dimensions of group action, which if followed characterize a "healthy" group which in turn produces healthy, mature individuals.

The Group Standard Dimension

All groups set standards affecting the behavior of their members. Sometimes these standards are unrealistic and people work under constant pressure trying to meet the standards established. In some families the standard for the children is to be like the oldest boy or girl. Younger children sometimes go through life trying to measure up to an unfortunate standard. Consider the college student who took five classes where each professor established the standard of two hours of homework for each hour in class. This was a physically unrealistic standard; and, as you all probably know students have ways of dealing with such conditions. They defend themselves by copying each other's work, cheating on exams, sharing assignments, trading book reports, and the list goes on.

I worked with one group of professional people who were having real difficulty meeting the standards they had established for themselves in a project. This was a volunteer project they were carrying out in addition to other duties. After some very probing meetings, they finally saw that for a few of the leaders of the project the groups' standards and goals were the most important matters on which they were working. For most of the others, this project ranked about fourth or fifth in importance in terms of other commitments. The leaders were pressuring for a set of standards that were very unrealistic for the others. Finally they worked out common standards of performance, time, and expense on which they could all agree and work without feelings of guilt and pressure.

If a person does not achieve the standards set by

the group, his self-esteem suffers. He may have real feelings of inadequacy or guilt. New students in a classroom, or new members of a community often run into standards of work and excellence for which they are unprepared, and they suffer from their in-adequacies. Groups need constantly to examine their standards to see if they are realistic in terms of the resources of the group members.

Groups also have at their command a kind of awe-some power to induce members to conform to their standards. Group members are rewarded by being accepted, included, and praised if they abide by the group norms, but are rejected, excluded, and ridiculed if they do not conform. How wonderful to be warmly accepted and included by others, and how terrible to be an outcast — rejected and ridiculed. The standards which allow acceptance or rejection often have no ob-jective validity. In one high school the standard for acceptance in the girls' cliques was the wearing of Jantzen skirts and sweaters. No other kind would do. The girls stood in a circle at the main entrance, and as the girls would come in, they would check the label in the neck of the sweater to see if it were a Jantzen. If it were, this girl was accepted. If not, she was not included in the circle. Some of the poorer girls came to the home economics teacher and asked if she would cut out the labels in her Jantzen sweaters so they could sew them in their sweaters and thus win acceptance. I wonder how many people there are who suffer from frustration, feelings of rejection, and feelings of inadequacy because for one reason or another they cannot measure up to various group standards equally as arbitrary as those of the girls.

The Involvement Dimension

The essence of the involvement principle is that people work most productively and happily when they are involved in establishing their own goals and pro-cedures. When all of the group members work together with a high degree of involvement in setting up what they are to do and how they are to do it, they

52

have a sense of commitment which is not present when the goals are imposed on them.

The late Kurt Lewin found that in decision making, where the group as a whole made the decision to have the group members change their method of operation, the results were from two to ten times more effective in situations where groups were asked to make changes as a result of lectures exhorting them to change.

In industry the results are striking. When groups are given the responsibility for their own goals and procedures, productivity and morale are increased.

Groups are often caught in an interesting dilemma in this matter of involvement in setting their own goals. On one hand people like to be involved and to participate in the planning for their own actions. On the other hand, when they are not used to doing this, or they run into conflict with people who have slightly different goals, or they cannot agree on procedures, it is often easier to rely on an authority who will tell them what to do and how to do it. Then it is the authority's job to keep after them to do the job, and it's his problem if the work doesn't get done. When we constantly turn to authorities to do this work for us, dependency gets reinforced. When people are not involved, they can belong to a group for years and never really participate.

The Authority of Leadership Dimension

Almost all formal groups and many informal ones have a recognized leader who represents something of a higher status, superior position, or greater power. It is important to see how these leaders function in the group and how the group members relate to the authority person.

In connection with the so-called aggressive child, we need to explore more fully the effects of group organization in producing aggressive action. Research has shown that when children who were aggressive in a group with one leadership style — namely authoritarian — were shifted to a group with a different

Almost all formal groups and many informal ones have a recognized leader.

leadership style — that of a democratic nature — the degree of aggressiveness shown in these children decreased markedly. Aggression perhaps must be seen in more than terms of personality traits. More exactly we have to see the personality as it operates within a particular type of group structure.

One study showed that the type of leadership pattern set by the teacher affected the behavior of the students. If the teacher were dominant in her contacts with the students, the students showed more compliance to as well as rejection of the teacher's domination. Also in these cases the students were more easily distracted from schoolwork, presumably because they spent more time worrying about the teacher than about the accomplishment of the work. Where the teacher was primarily helpful and tried to integrate the students into class activities, there was more spontaneity, initiative, voluntary social helping of student to student, and more effective problem solving.

Along this same line, another study showed that better classroom attitudes exist where the students have greater opportunity to express their own ideas and feelings. The teachers would more often ask questions about the student's feelings, and would praise, encourage, and accept the student's ideas and feelings in a nonthreatening way. Those classrooms with a less desirable feeling found the teacher spending most of the time lecturing, giving directions and criticism. I am sure that these findings in the classroom are true of most other groups.

Commonly people relate to the authority person in one of three ways: Either they are very dependent on the leader, are hostile or counter dependent, or are interdependent, that is, they can work with the leader in a cooperative way. Some leaders like people to be dependent and encourage this; some leaders are so task oriented they do not see the counterreactions to them that drain off the energies and creativity and emotional well-being of the members. Hopefully we in leadership positions center our focus on the people and their needs and try to create conditions which allow us work *with* them rather than over them.

The Feedback Dimension

Here we draw a term from the field of engineering. Feedback in a guided missile is the process whereby electronic computers guiding the missile detect when the missile is going off course and feedback data into the direction device which allows the missile to get back on the right track.

Groups and individuals need to have a similar type of mechanism; that is, some way of finding out when they are behaving in ways that are seen as "off the track" so they can find out what they need to do to get back on the right course again.

It is not easy either to give or to receive feedback. People are reluctant to tell others their mistakes, i.e., the bad breath ad which states that "even your best friends won't tell you." Also people who are told they are "off the track" often react in very defensive ways, for they need to protect themselves. A common reaction when someone tells us our errors is to attack him and point out all his faults.

Groups need to develop the kind of climate or atmosphere in which feedback can be expressed with the real understanding that it is given in a helpful way. More groups need to have some way of looking at what they are doing and getting some evaluation and feedback on how the group is working. Individuals and groups can err. If they are to improve, they need to know their errors. This needs to be done in such a way that the persons involved are not damaged, but helped.

The Climate or Atmosphere Dimension

The emotional climate or atmosphere is very real yet very difficult to measure. We do know that people are affected dramatically by the emotional milieu within which they must live. We talk most often about the permissive or accepting climate in contrast to the defensive or rejecting climate. We have all been in situations where the climate was cold or formal or fun or reflective or sad. We are simply describing the prevailing mood of the group. We've all been in a group or been with a group where everything seemed to go right. It's such a good feeling that we hate to see the meeting or activity come to a close.

What are some of the ingredients that go into creating the type of climate that produces this type of healthy well-being? I have already mentioned above some of the factors — involvement of the total group in the problem at hand, adequate and helpful group standards, leaders who work *with* not *over*, and a healthy feedback system. Here are some other things to consider.

An Attitude of Acceptance of Others Different from Ourselves

We are not all cut from the same cloth, and we need to learn to accept others for what they have to contribute. Acceptance of others does not mean we have to like everyone on an intimate basis. We can learn to appreciate others and their ideas even though they are quite different from ourselves. In one study, a group of managers were asked first, "Who do you like best in the organization?" and they listed their choices. Then they were asked "Who has the best ideas in the organization?"; as we might suspect, they listed the same choices. I'm sure that most of us really know that the people we like are not all brilliant, creative, sensitive, and so on. But how often do we let our feelings of like distort our perceptions of the worth of other persons.

Real, Not Pretended, Interest

Some interesting studies have shown that people can readily detect persons who are sincerely interested in others in contrast to persons who are only pretending an interest. We have all shuddered at the hearty, "Well, how are we today" given us by doctors, salesmen, and others who assume a professional but not a real interest. In one study of a hospital ward the patients were asked with whom they talked over their important problems. The professional staff were greatly surprised when the patients listed such persons as the janitor, the elevator boy, one's mother, the patient in the next bed. In the seventy-five interviews made, there was not a single mention of a nurse or one of the professional people working with the patients.

I wonder if we asked students where they get help how many would mention parents or teachers? People can tell if others really accept them and are interested in them. Data also show that people can *learn* to be more accepting of others.

Honest Approval and Disapproval

People like to work and live in situations where they are approved for work well done and told honestly and fairly when work is below par. Too often we assume that people we are close to — family, friends, colleagues — know that we approve of and like them. I am interested in the number of times I hear about wives who ask, "Dear, do you really love me? You never tell." A usual answer is "You ought to know I love you. I married you, didn't I?" I am constantly amazed as I talk with young people how many of them are not really sure that their parents love them.

In giving praise and criticism we have to be careful about the use of the so-called sandwich technique. This is the slipping of a piece of criticism between two slices of praise. "John, you did a real fine job last week, BUT, I want to talk to you about what you did yesterday." What this does is rob the praise from any impact. Every time he hears praise he begins to stiffen for the blow he knows will come.

Listening Instead of Always Telling

We are all aware that communication is part telling and part listening, but often our listening skills are very low.

Allowing People to Make Mistakes

In a defensive climate people usually spend their time trying to defend themselves against the authority persons. They do not have time or emotional energy to be creative — to grow and mature — for their energies are dissipated in trying to protect themselves from the punishment, censoring, telling, controlling efforts of others. To the degree we can create the type of accepting, permissive group atmosphere, we will be moving toward the direction of improving the emotional health and maturity of the individual.

The Task-Feeling Level Dimension

One of the most significant findings of research on groups has been the recognition of two levels of group action. Most groups meet together for a particular task or problem-solving purpose. A committee formed to improve conditions relative to mental health in a school has a specific task to accomplish. But we have also discovered that people, like machines, cannot work indefinitely on a task without some maintenance taking place. People get tired, angry, frustrated, apathetic, tense, and so forth, while they are working together on the problem. Too often

in groups we try to ignore all of these feelings and
needs that are in a state of disrepair and to move all
the more quickly to finishing the task before the
group blows up. The assumption is that just getting
the group to agree on the action to be taken is all that
is needed. But we know that if the feeling level has
been neglected and people do not feel happy about
the group and its work they are ineffective in carrying
out their assignments, they stay away from meetings,
and they are tremendously relieved when the committee finally disbands.

It is *not* a waste of time for groups to take time to
ensure that misunderstandings are cleared, to relieve
tension, visit and relax, tell jokes, and exchange personal experiences. These are some of the maintenance
functions going on which keep the group in a state of
health so it can accomplish its task. We live in a
task-oriented society where the emphasis is on more
and more production. We neglect the feelings and
emotions of people at our own peril.

These are some of the important dimensions of
group life that have serious implications for individual
development and mental health. The groups we
belong to are major determining forces in shaping
our likes and dislikes, establishing our goals and our
methods for achieving them, determining what prej-
udices and attitudes we should hold, and shaping our
overall maturity and health. We need to tap the resources of group life for our continuing benefit.

Reference

Argyris, Chris
    1957   Personality and Organization. New York: Harper
          and Row, Publishers.

Feedback *

Probably no activity is more widely used and less understood than the process of interpersonal feedback, particularly as it has been articulated in the current laboratory training movement which is variously called T-Groups, encounter groups, sensitivity groups, and so on. It would seem that these various forms of data sharing would have differing impacts on others, and perhaps by clarifying the processes it may be possible for persons to develop greater skill in engaging in a most needed activity.

Feedback is a process of data sharing where a person receives *from others* information about his own behavioral performance. There are two parts to feedback: (1) the giving of data about the nature of the behavior, usually describing the behavior as a person sees or experiences it; and (2) the sharing of information with the person as to how the receiver felt about or responded to the behavior. The sharing of feedback data is not a new process, only a new term is being used. Only recently has the process come under serious scrutiny to see what kinds of feedback lead to the most beneficial interpersonal results. Following are the types of feedback that we commonly experience.

Types of Feedback

Objective-Descriptive

This is a process of trying to describe as clearly and objectively as possible the behaviors one has seen another person utilize. This is feedback only in the first part defined above; it does not tell a person the effect his behavior has had on others, but it is a reporting back to the person that gives a description of his behavior as seen by an observer. Following are examples of this type of feedback:

"You only spoke three times during the last hour."

"When you talk, you look only at the trainer, never at anyone else."

---

*Revised. Reprinted by special permission from Journal for American Society of Training Directors, "Forms of interpersonal feedback," William G. Dyer 26 (July 1972).

60

"When you talk, you always look down or away, but never directly at the person you are talking to."

"When you talk, you always look down or away, but never directly at the person you are talking to."

"You tried to get into the conversation four times but never succeeded and then you didn't try again."

This type of feedback attempts to give a person a mirror image of what his behavior is like. We are often not aware of the behaviors we utilize, and the purpose of this type of feedback generally is to help the person more clearly look at his own behavior.

A careful observer, through this feedback process, can help another person look at his behavior more carefully. An observer might tell a manager or group leader that at his last meeting Mr. Allen raised his hand three times but the leader ignored him. Or he might point out that the leader cut two people off, contradicted or rejected the contributions of three others, rephrased a proposition that had been made in his own language so it was different from the original, and then pressed for a vote when others said they still wanted to discuss. Such a description might be very helpful to the person receiving the data, even though he did not get any information about how anyone actually felt about his performance. The receiver of the feedback is left to ponder about the possible consequences or impacts of his behavior on others, or the observer may report some consequential data such as, "When you ignored Mr. Allen, I saw him pick up a paper and read it throughout the rest of the meeting; he never contributed again." The observer might also engage in another type of feedback.

Assumed or Guessed Impact

This type of feedback shows the assumptions or the guesses by a second-party observer as to what he, the observer, thinks or guesses the impact of the person's behavior is. Some examples of this type of feedback would be:

"I think you hurt Mary's feelings. I saw her crying after you scolded her."

"I think that there is a lot of hostility and resent-

ment toward you as a result of the way you conducted the meeting."

"If I were Joe, I would really be angry with you if you treated me the way you did him."

The person receiving this type of feedback may find this helpful, for he may not have detected how people were feeling about his behavior. But it is also nonvalidated feedback; it is only a guess as to how people feel and think. A sensitive, insightful observer may be able to pick up feelings of others to a close degree, but it is not the same as getting direct data from the object of the behavior. The direct feedback process allows the possibility of working through some differences not possible in the second-party guess, but such guessed impact may give the person receiving the feedback some clues about what he may want to do about his behavior in the future, or may suggest some actions to be taken to check out the actual impact on the person involved.

Second-Party Report of Impact

From time to time a person may receive feedback about the impact of his behavior on others, but it comes from someone other than the direct recipient of the behavior. It is a second-party report of data that he has received from someone else. It can also be reported directly to the person.

"Tom told me that he was afraid to come into your office, for he always feels that you put him on the spot."

"I talked with someone (I can't mention names) who told me that he felt very upset with the way you hog the limelight at staff meetings."

Second-party data has some built-in difficulties, although it may be perfectly accurate. First, there is always the possibility that it is not being reported exactly as the other person experienced it. Second, it is not possible to interact directly with the person to work through any difficulties. Such opportunities must be set up later. Third, the person reporting the data may be uneasy about the confidentiality problem.

While the person who had the experience may not have directly said not to report it, the second party doesn't know if he can legitimately tell who said it. Then the person receiving the feedback doesn't know if he can respond directly when the data he has received has come through a second party.

Direct Descriptive Impact

Most people who have written about feedback have postulated that this may be the most useful form of feedback. This is a descriptive process, first describing the person's behavior and then describing other's reactions to that behavior. This is done directly between the persons involved.

"When you yelled at me just now, it made me feel very hostile and resentful toward you."

"When you supported me on that motion, I felt very appreciative and good toward you."

The advantage of this form is that it gives the person receiving the feedback a clear picture of his behavior and what effect or impact that behavior has on others. When given directly, it often opens up the opportunity to deal directly with the person and to have a chance to work out a resolution of any difficulty. This direct feedback must also be accompanied by such conditions as a climate of trust and concern, a desire to improve the relationship, time to work on the issue, and complementary expectations that such feedback is appropriate and desirable. However, if stated in the direct descriptive terms, it shares the data in a way that allows the person to work most easily with the information.

Sometimes we get feedback that is descriptive but represents only part of the total descriptive formula.

"I feel very uneasy with you."

"You make me feel inferior and stupid."

The person receiving the feedback knows how the person feels about him, but he does not know exactly what kind of behavior produces the feelings. It is difficult to know what one can do to alter the feelings in others.

When in the process of human interaction one person responds to the behavior of another, then it is often an evaluation or judgment one attaches to the behavior. Much feedback is in the form of a sharing of the evaluations or judgments one makes as a result of the behavior.

"You are really a rigid, authoritarian person."

"I think you are a cold fish."

"I find you a very selfish person."

If feedback is given at step 3, then descriptive feedback may result. If feedback is given at step 4, it represents one's judgments. When people first try to give feeling-descriptive feedback, it sometimes turns out like this, "Joe, when you push your ideas through at the meeting I feel like you are a real dictator."

Even though the person uses the words "I feel like . . .," he really is expressing his evaluation of the behavior. A person feels angry, hostile, jealous,

Sequence of feedback

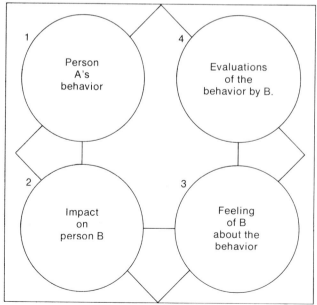

uneasy, affectionate, tender. At least these are words we use to try to describe the emotional state inside us. We don't feel like someone is a dictator. This is a result of our thinking processes and represents a judgment of the behavior one has experienced.

Evaluative feedback may be very important data to receive, for it is sometimes difficult to know exactly why a person feels so upset unless we know how he has evaluated the behavior. There is apparently a connection between our feelings and our evaluations, and knowing the evaluation is a key to understanding and feelings. If Bill thinks that people who initiate often, talk a great deal, and push for decisions are controlling, regulating, authoritarian types of people, then he will resent such actions. Hal experiencing the same behavior will see such actions as helpful and facilitative. Thus a key to working out a relationship would be to understand Bill's evaluation of the behavior.

Direct Expressive

Feedback comes sometimes in the form of direct expressions of feeling about the total person.
"I really like you."
"I distrust you."
It seems that people sometimes respond to the total person and have feelings that are generalized about the person. When we think about this, the general statements are probably seldom if ever completely true. A person who says, "I like you," probably does not mean that he likes everything about the other person, just as a dislike reaction doesn't mean one dislikes everything about the other. However, these generalized feelings are important, for we probably experience and react quite differently to a person we have a general feeling of liking toward than to a person we have general dislike feelings toward.

If one is going to alter general negative feelings, it is probably important that he move the feedback into the more specific, descriptive area. He needs to know more concretely and specifically what he is doing that creates the negative reaction.

Nonverbal

Data are often returned to a person in terms of the nonverbal cues he picks up from others. We see people smile, frown, turn away, fidget, turn pale or livid, or yawn as we interact with them. We see this as feedback about their reactions to us, and some people are very sensitive to nonverbal cues, some insensitive, and others hypersensitive.

One must always be cautious in interpreting nonverbal feedback, for the meaning of the nonverbal reaction may vary from person to person, in fact between sender and receiver. When Bill nods his head, he may mean that he has heard the message, but Hal may interpret this as meaning agreement and support.

One person may frown and grimace when he is thoughtful or challenged by the ideas of another, but the other person may see this as a sign of rejection. Since nonverbal cues are open to interpretation, they should probably be checked out with the sender and feedback of a more specific type should be elicited.

Performance Reactions

Nonverbal cues as described above are limited body cues that people give off in response to others. We can also receive certain performance cues that give us feedback about the effect of our behavior. The manager who finds that a subordinate is carrying out an assignment in a way quite the opposite from what the manager thought he said is getting feedback that his instructions were not clear or at least were not understood as he intended.

Again, these performance cues are initial feedback indications that things may not be going as we intended. We can learn from the performance cues that we may need to move the feedback process into a more intensive, descriptive level.

Nonverbal cues are limited body cues that people give off in response to others.

A feedback method that has long been employed by many organizations is the use of systematic data collection devices such as questionnaires, surveys, evaluation forms, and interviews. There are certain advantages and disadvantages to these methods. The tabulated responses give the person a picture of the reactions of many people to him. A manager may be able to see that ten of his fifteen subordinates feel that he spends almost no time in sharing information about changes that occur in the organization. It is also possible to gather some feeling data about a person's performance.

I have a strong personal reaction to John when

1. He makes me feel angry or dominated.
2. He makes me feel involved and excited.
3. He makes me feel guilty or ashamed.
4. He makes me feel outmaneuvered or off-balance.

Many volumes have been written on methods of data collection, survey research, interviewing, scale construction, and others. It is not appropriate to review all those here. It is important, however, that when instrumented methods are used that skill and care are used in developing valid and reliable procedures. Regardless of the accuracy of the collected data, there is always a limitation to this form of feedback as a means of improvement. The collected data are often cold and impersonal, and there is no real communication of the actual feelings involved. Just receiving the data does not connect the person *receiving* the data with the person or persons *giving* the data, and does not allow the possibility of working through differences. This is always a possibility in direct face-to-face feedback sessions. Instrumented feedback is really just the beginning of a process for working on resolving differences between people.

Functions of Feedback

The above formulation describes various types of feedback that people often share with each other. A critical factor that influences the impact that the feedback has on the other person is the motivation of the person giving the data. A person giving feedback to someone else should also examine not only his method but his motivation. The form may be correct, but if the motivation is to punish or put down the other person, the impact may not be positive. Following are some of the major reasons why people give feedback to others.

To Punish, Hurt, or Put Down

When we are angry, hurt, or defensive, we may respond to the person or persons who have wounded us by giving feedback with the intent to get even or to hurt or wound as we have been hurt. Evaluative feedback is probably most often used in such cases, but almost any type of feedback might be used.

"You are nothing but a snob, and nobody I know likes you."

"You make me sick; I just can't stand working with you."

"I know how you have been trying to do a good job, but frankly you are just incompetent."

Feedback can also be given by changing the voice inflection and thus communicating a completely different message. Consider: "Thanks a lot; that was really a helpful suggestion." The phrase could be varying. The inflection could be used either to praise and support, or to punish and put down. The person giving feedback should be aware of his own motivations and not pretend one motivation set when other feelings are really prompting his behavior.

To Reward and Support

Supportive or rewarding feedback is important not only in reinforcing behaviors we want to persist in others but in improving our relationships. Such feedback may also be just a spontaneous expression of good feeling toward another person.

"That was a great idea."

"When you supported my position, I really felt good and I appreciated it."

"Nobody I know likes you!"

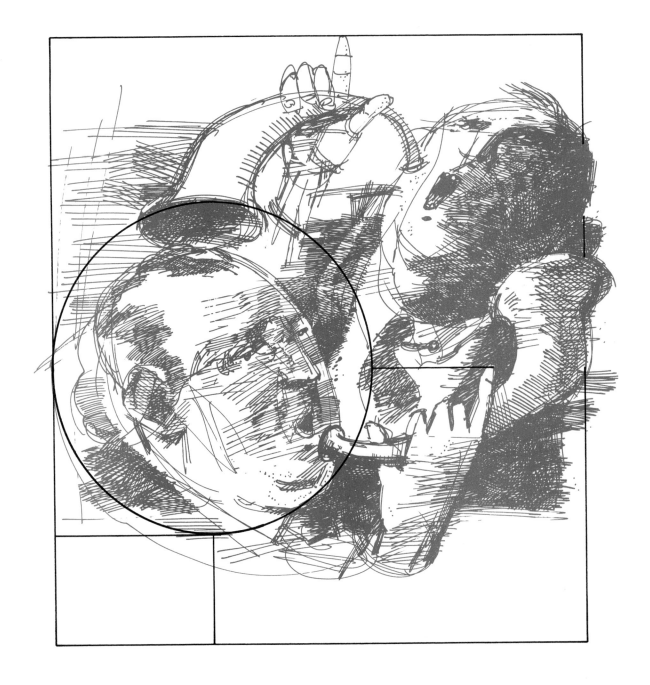

"I just want you to know that I like you and appreciate your work."

It would seem that such positive feedback would be most welcomed and people would want to hear such reactions. However, there are people who find it very difficult to share such feedback with others, and there are also people who accept such feedback reluctantly and some who are always suspicious of the motives of people who give them supportive data.

To Help Another Improve His Performance

A common motivation stemming from current training programs is the sharing of feedback data out of a desire to help another person improve his effectiveness in his interactions with others. Out of this motivation, the feedback could either be considered positive or negative, but both are accepted because the person receiving the data feels that it is given in a spirit of helpfulness. One commonly hears a person in a training setting wanting to hear only the negative or critical feedback, for he has confidence that the people are trying to be helpful and he wants to know those behaviors that are creating problems for him.

To Improve One's Relationships

Feedback can also be a means of opening up some areas of difficulties between persons and beginning a process of improving the relationship.

"I've been worried about our relationship. I've felt you have been avoiding me, and I would like to talk about it."

"John, I've noticed you have been disagreeing with me almost constantly and that really bothers me. What's going on between us?"

Consequences of Feedback

It should be recognized that just the giving of data in the form of feedback is no guarantee that conditions will improve. Feedback may result in individuals either improving their relationships with each other or in appropriate change in behavior or perceptions

(Dyer, 1969). However, if people are not skillful or if they do not stay in the situation and deal with the consequences of the feedback, interpersonal situations may worsen (Thibaut and Coules, 1952:770-777).

The ultimate consequence of feedback is to allow people to engage in a process of data sharing in such a way that greater effectiveness in interpersonal behavior results. Some types of feedback seem to facilitate adjustment, harmony, and mutual acceptance more easily than do other forms.

Different people may have developed a certain preference for one type of feedback. It may be important for them to see which forms they use and which forms are more useful. It should also be mentioned that a good training program to help people examine their own style of feedback and to practice better forms has not yet been developed.

References

Dyer, William G.
   1969   "Acceptance or change." Human Relations Training News 13.

Thibaut, John W., and John Coules
   1952   "The role of communications in the reduction of interpersonal hostility." Journal of Abnormal and Social Psychology 47:770-777.

Following the first wave of contact and interaction and the initial impact of people on one another comes one of the most common occurrences in a training group — the giving of feedback, or letting a person know the effect his behavior has had on others. It can almost be predicted that certain kinds of behaviors will elicit the first attempts at feedback: the silent or relatively nonverbal group member, the highly aggressive or structuring performance, the overtalker, the caustic or sarcastic remark.

Implicit in the feedback process seems to be the notion of change — change in the person receiving the feedback. Feedback to one of the behaviors above goes something like this:

Sam: "Tom, you haven't said anything much at all for the last two sessions. I get quite anxious when you don't say anything. Why don't you speak up more? I really listen whenever you say something."

Tom: "I speak up whenever I feel I have anything to contribute. I'm really a quiet person, and I just don't talk very much in groups this size."

Sam is giving what is appropriate feedback. He is telling Tom the effect his behavior has on others, and he does this in a descriptive, nonjudgmental way. Still there is a basic request for Tom to change. If Tom finds out that his quiet behavior makes others anxious, he must feel a certain pressure to change his performance and to increase the quantity of his verbal contributions. It would seem that Tom could legitimately respond to the feedback this way:

Tom: "If my quietness bothers you, why don't you change? Why can't you learn to accept quiet people like me? Why do I have to change to make you feel better?"

This presents the hub of a real dilemma on the interaction scene. If Tom's behavior "bothers" Sam (or a number of other persons), what should be the goal of the subsequent interaction?

*Revised. Reprinted by special permission from Human Relations Training News, "Acceptance or change," William G. Dyer 13 (1969).

1. Should Sam give feedback to Tom with the expectation that he should engage in some type of behavior change?

2. Should Sam assume that it is his own problem and try to expand his acceptance of Tom's behavior without giving him any feedback?

Within this dichotomy are a number of ramifications of the issue: Are there some types of behaviors that are so deeply a part of a person's "personality" — so fixed and deep-rooted that change is almost impossible? If such be the case, what are these kinds of behaviors? If we could identify them, it would seem that persons who encounter such unchangeable behaviors should concentrate on widening their margin of acceptance rather than expecting such persons to engage in behavior change. Exactly what types of behavior can be changed is difficult to assess. From my experience in groups, I recall a number of situations which presented behaviors that posed a dilemma for the group.

Fred had a facial grimace that appeared when he became tense or anxious in the group. To others it seemed to be a sneer, and it was interpreted that he was somewhat disdainful of others and the problems that where being discussed. This became the focus of a great deal of early feedback to Fred. He claimed that this was a facial pattern which had been a part of his reactions as long as he could remember. He said he did not feel disdainful, but he knew that he looked that way to others. Thereafter the group assumed that this was something he could not change and that they should try to understand and accept it.

June was a quiet member. She said she was "just naturally" a quiet person and did not speak up much in a group setting. Other group members did not accept this, and she was constantly encouraged to try to change her behavior. It seemed that some group members took it as a challenge to get June to become more vocal.

Alice was told that people experienced her as a

rather cold and distant person. Group members felt they could not relate easily to her and were not drawn to her. She was contrasted to Mary, who was seen as a very warm, friendly person whom people liked and enjoyed. There was the direct inference that if Alice could be more like Mary she would be a more effective person.

Tom was "blasted" in the first round of feedback for his constant attempts to get the group "organized." He had pushed hard to get the group to identify its goals, to set up some type of agenda of activities, and to start working and not just sit around discussing "whatever happens to come up." Tom said he was the kind of person who worked better when things were organized, but the group said he pushed too hard, and they resented his attempts to structure them.

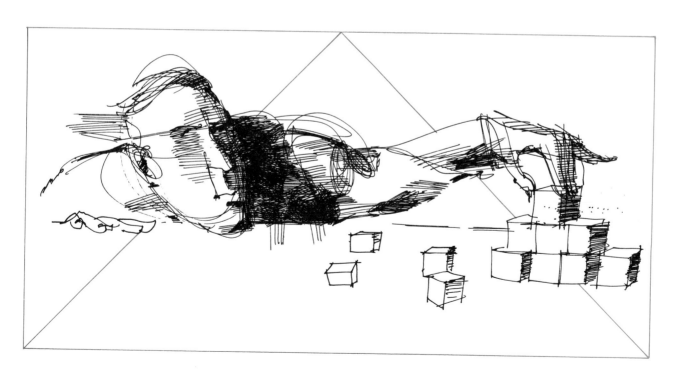

Kathy was told that she seemed to avoid any conflict in the group. She was seen as always trying to smooth over difficulties. It appeared that she agreed with people quickly and seemed to avoid any confrontation with anyone. Kathy claimed that she was the type of person who liked to get along with people. She said she did not like arguments and discord and would rather go along with something she did not agree with in order to avoid conflict.

All of the above are real situations and have been replicated to a certain degree many times over in various groups that I have observed. Which of the above types represent behaviors that can or ought to be changed?

A common stance taken in training is that we should be open with our feelings and give feedback about whatever our reactions happen to be. But what is the function of the feedback? What is its purpose and how do we respond to it? If Sam gives Tom feedback about behavior that "bothers" Sam, what stance does Sam adopt while waiting for Tom to decide whether he wants to or can change? Does Sam just accept Tom the way he is whether he changes or not? If that is the case, why does Sam give Tom feedback at all — why not just accept Tom the way he already is?

And what about Tom? Having been given feedback about his behavior, what should he now do? He knows that Sam is bothered; if he doesn't change, how is Sam going to feel about him? Is he sitting back waiting for some sign of change?

Acceptance seems to imply accepting a person the way he is, not the way we should like him to be. It could be argued that if we accept a person the way he is and this is the essential condition for building trust and subsequently working together then the basic process in human interaction is one of constantly expanding one's own margin of acceptance of others. Feedback, in the sense of implying change, seems to be superfluous. If feedback implying change is a basic interaction process, then what is it about

What is the function of feedback?

the other person we accept? If we accept some things and not others, what determines the one over the other?

Here we face an important matter of values. What one does or does not accept in the behavior of others depends, in part, on what one values, what is considered appropriate, right, acceptable. If a person engages in behaviors that we find nonacceptable, it would seem that we should begin to examine our value system to see whether it is possible to alter the values upon which the reaction is based. If that is not possible, we may then need to engage in some kind of feedback process which leads to the working out of some behavior change.

What kinds of behaviors in the examples given above would represent unacceptable behaviors — behaviors that would violate a basic value? For myself, the two case situations that would have some value implications for me would be Tom and Kathy. If Tom were the type of person who wanted to control people, wanted to impose his ideas and opinions on others, this would violate a basic value for me. Tom might see himself as just being "well organized," but, if I experienced him as one who was trying to control my thinking or actions, I would need to engage in some direct feedback process and work on the issue between us.

Kathy may see herself as just a pleasant person who likes to get along with people, but, if I experienced her as a person who held her feelings inside and did not share them and pretended to behave in ways inconsistent with her feelings, this would violate a value for me and would lead to my initiating feedback to her.

For behavior that I initially experience as "bothersome," I should try to examine my own values and see whether I need to try to expand my margin of acceptance or whether the behavior hits at an area important enough to be raised in the process of feedback. At that point I should be the one to initiate the feedback. In the T-Group I have often responded to a request for feedback and have shared negative feelings even when they did not violate a value. When the other person initiates a request for feedback, I feel that he has a right to find out how his behavior effects others, and my values would lead me to share the data that I have about him. If he asks me how I experience him, I should want to give him the feedback data and also tell him whether the behavior just "bothers" me or whether I experience it as a violation of certain basic values for me.

Feedback, then, is not just a request for change in behavior but a beginning of the process of acceptance or change, if needed. I have often seen a T-Group give a person a great deal of feedback and a few days later comment to that person how much change they had experienced in him. Probably an outside observer would have detected very little actual behavior change. Interestingly enough, following the feedback session the previous "bothersome" behavior was no longer such a source of irritation, even though the person had probably not changed much. This suggests to me that one of the critical functions of feedback is the beginning of the process of acceptance. It seems that we can accept behavior much more readily if we can talk about it openly and the person receiving the feedback accepts it — that is, he is willing to hear it and take it into account. This seems to be the start of accepting behavior between the persons involved. I am thus defining feedback as not just a process of requesting a person to change but the beginning of the process of wider acceptance of each other.

The forming of a new family constitutes a major behavioral change for a young man and woman, since they now occupy new roles. Most people are new to these roles and are inexperienced in adapting themselves to the demands of continually interacting with other personalities. Role theory allows us to more clearly outline and understand the forms of adjustment that these persons in their new roles usually need to make.[1]

Role Expectations

Each marriage partner enters marriage with certain ideas as to how he should behave in his new position, but each also has certain expectations as to how the other person should behave in his (the other's) role. Role expectations, then, are the ways one person feels the other should behave (Parsons, 1951:38). In terms of the new marriage relationship, the new husband has some ideas as to how he should behave as a husband (his role) and he also has some idea as to how his wife should behave in her role (his role expectations of his wife). Conversely the wife has some definition of her role and certain expectations of her husband's role.

One problem in the matter of role behavior is focused in the question of role definitions versus role performance. There is often a difference between what is agreed on as to what one *should* do and what one *actually* does. A husband and wife could both agree that it is part of the husband's role to plan and carry out the recreational activities of the growing boys in the family. In actuality the husband does not do this. It could be maintained that the husband's role is what he actually does in his position, but the expectations of the wife appear, at least at first in the marriage, to be derived from the definition of be-

---

*Revised. Reprinted by special permission from Marriage and Family Living, "Analyzing marital adjustment using role theory," Willaim G. Dyer 24 (November 1962):371-375.

[1] For a more extensive treatment of these elements, see Newcomb (1950), chapters 8, 9, 10, 14, and 15.

havior that is agreed on between them.

In marriage each partner probably starts out with certain expectations as to how husbands or wives in general ought to behave, and these generalized expectations are applied to the specific behavior of the other partner. Later, part of the expectations may be altered to include the specialized expectation of specific role elements derived out of their experience together. For example, at first a wife may expect her husband to be a general handyman around the house (derived from her generalized expectations) and is disappointed when he prefers to golf. Later an agreement may be reached that he must at least mow the lawn, wash the car, and replace used light bulbs. If the husband does no "handyman" type jobs at all, he is violating a generalized expectation. If he fails to take out the garbage, he is not meeting a specifically agreed on expectation.

It should be pointed out that each partner usually has not only expectations of *what* should be done by the other but also *how* the particular function should be carried out. The wife may not only expect her husband to share in the household tasks but to do it in a cooperative, pleasant manner. Her expectations can be violated should he not perform the task or if he does it in a surly, unpleasant way.

A. R. Mangus (1957:256-62) in his article on mental health in the family, using a theoretical orientation very similar to the one used here, points out that expectations may also be centered around a concept of the marriage partner as a total personality. Each partner usually has not only expectations of what and how the other person should behave in his role, but also how the other person should be as a person. Conflicts may come when one's self-perception does not agree with the perception of the marriage partner. The husband may see himself as efficient, helpful, and friendly while his wife sees him as stingy, suspicious, and overbearing. If the wife expects her husband to be a certain kind of personality, his behavior, manifesting symptoms of a contrary type, will elicit negative reactions from her. The problem is intensified when he cannot understand why she sees him this way because he sees himself so differently.

An important part of this analysis is to try to see expectations as attached to specific role functions rather than becoming generalized around the total person. If a wife sees her husband as a certain kind of person, this may distort her perceptions of him in all his role performances. Under these circumstances, adjustment in the sense to be described below may be difficult to achieve, for it is uncertain that the change of role performance on the part of the husband will alter her perceptions of him as a total person, although it may be argued that alterations in role performance may be the most effective way for the wife to develop a new conception of her husband.

Sanctions

Sanctions are the rewards or punishments administered by one person to another to the degree the other person meets or fails to meet his role expectations. In the family situation, if the husband's performance in his role meets the wife's role expectations, she will generally apply positive sanctions or rewards such as praise, affection, and good will. If his role performance violates her expectations, she will often apply negative sanctions, tears, quarreling, or withdrawal of affection.

Generally human interactions move along most smoothly if the following conditions exist: (1) if the parties interacting have a high level of agreement on norms and personal preferences, (2) if the parties involved agree as to the role definitions and role expectations of each other, (3) if the role performance of one is in agreement with the role expectations of the other, and positive sanctions are the end result of the interaction.

Marriage Adjustment

We may now consider marriage adjustment:

Points of Conflict

Conflicts in the marriage situation may arise at the following places in terms of the above schema:

1. If the norms and personal preferences of the husband are in conflict with those of the wife.

2. If the role performance of the husband does not agree with the role expectations of the wife.

3. If the role performance of the wife does not agree with the role expectations of the husband.

In each of the above cases dissatisfaction with the marriage relationship may occur with a resulting application of negative sanctions. Negative sanctions may be directly or indirectly applied, or these feelings of dissatisfaction may be repressed or directed toward someone or something else.

Possible Methods of Adjustment

In each of the above conflict situations, there are certain kinds of adjustments available:

1. In conflict point one, the couple needs to clarify to each other their norms or personal preferences so that each knows exactly the point of view of the other. This of necessity involves mature and extensive communication. To the degree the disparity between norms is translated into role performance, the following adjustments would be more applicable.

2. In conflict situations two and three, the possibility of adjustment is the same:

a. The husband (or wife) can change his role performance completely to meet the role expectations of his partner.

b. The husband (or wife) can change his role expectations completely to coincide with the role performance of the partner.

c. There can be a mutual adjustment, each partner altering some. The husband (or wife) can alter his role performance to a degree, and the partner alters her role expectations to a similar degree so that role performance and role expectations are compatible. In each of the above cases the end result is an agreement between role performance and role expectations.

3. There is also another type of adjustment possible. In some cases the couple might recognize a disparity between role performance and role expectations or between norms and also acknowledge that change is difficult or impossible and could "agree to disagree." In such cases the one partner recognizes and respects the position of the other without accepting or adjusting to it. This pattern of "agreeing to disagree" is not adjustment in the same sense as the others listed above. The "adjustment" comes from both partners agreeing that a certain area is "out of bounds" as far as the application of sanctions is concerned. There is no change in behavior but some change in expectations in that each now expects certain areas not to be raised as issues and that no sanctions will be applied over these out-of-bound issues. This type of adjustment may be possible in certain areas of married life, but some areas may be too vital to the relationship not to have reached one of the other types of adjustment.

Some Problems in Adjustment

Public Versus Private Adjustment

The above model emphasizes the actual outward, public behavior of the couple as the essence of adjustment. Complete adjustment would be obtained only if the change in behavior were accompanied by a mental state of "feeling good" about the change in behavior. If a husband changed his role performance

to meet his wife's expectations publicly, adjustment would appear to occur, but privately he could resent "giving in" to her and transfer this resentment into areas other than that around which the "adjustment" took place.[2]

The Need for Feedback

An almost universal element in the process of change of social behavior is that of feedback. It is difficult, if not impossible, for one partner to know exactly how he is violating the expectations of the other, if the other does not respond with adequate feedback. Often feedback cues are given out by one partner but the other may misread the cues, misinterpret them, or deny them, if the feedback is not stated clearly in an atmosphere of acceptance when the climate is not "defensive" (Gibb, 1959). This open communication of expectations and feedback about the degree the other has met, or failed to meet, these expectations is often extremely difficult for newly marrieds. There are fears that, "If I give feedback to the other person I may lose the level of warmth and affection we now have," or fear that the other may retaliate. People are also inhibited from giving feedback by feelings of inadequacy as to how to proceed, lack of what might be an appropriate time, or feelings that one is not really sure he is "right" about his own criticism of the partner.

Often one learns of the expectations of others and how he has or has not met these expectations only via a trial-and-error method or in a sudden outburst of feeling when the other feels "I can't take it any

---

[2]In testing a similar phenomena, Kelman (1956) distinguishes between *compliance* (the adopting of a new behavior not because one believes in its content, but because he expects to gain specific rewards of approval and avoid specific punishments or disapproval); *identification* (the adopting of new behavior because it is associated with the desired relationship); and *internalization* (the adopting of a new behavior because one finds it useful for the solution of a problem or because it is congenial to his needs).

longer."[3] Neither of these conditions of feedback encourages the opportunity for mutual sharing of data in an atmosphere of helpfulness where the feedback has the best opportunity of being perceived as being helpful to the total relationship.

Adjustment Versus "Making Up"

Adjustment has been discussed above in terms of bringing into agreement the behavior of one person with the expectations of another, accompanied by a feeling of acceptance of the modified behavior by the one who makes the adjustment. A phenomena recognized in many cases of marital discord is the subsequent process of "making up." This is usually a process of repairing the feeling of unity and cohesion.

From an examination of a number of case studies it appears entirely possible for a couple to make up without achieving any adjustment in the sense described above. The violation of expectations often results in a feeling of discord and hostility between the couple. In a moment of mutual sympathy and regret for past actions, the couple may seek each other's forgiveness and "kiss and make up." This puts them back in a harmonious relationship with each other, but since no modification of either expectation or behavior has occurred, the disruption may occur again.

"Kiss and make up."

It is also possible for adjustment to occur without a resulting repairing of the emotional state of unity. It would seem that this would occur less frequently, particularly if there were also a private feeling of adjustment, since the result of the mutual agreement of expectation and behavior should be a response of positive sanction.

In terms of reinforcement learning theory it seems essential that a modification of either expectations or behavior on the part of one partner be rewarded by the other (Miller and Dollard 1941). One not only

[3]This trial-and-error learning is similar to what has been called *operant conditioning* — the subtle learning of subjects to respond to reinforcing stimuli (Verplanch, 1957:127-36).

needs to find out what one does wrong, but also what one does right. The continual giving of positive sanctions may be a necessary part of marital adjustment.

Role Conflict and Adjustment

Basic to the problem of role conflict is the paradoxical condition that in performing a role the same response brings *both* reward and punishment. A strongly religious wife who meets her husband's expectations by going skiing with him on Sunday may violate the expectations she and others may hold about her role as a church member. The response of going skiing brings both reward and punishment — reward from husband and punishment from self through feelings of self-recrimination of having violated another role one has internalized.

A marital partner may also find himself in conflict because of differing expectations as to how his role should be carried out. The young wife may discover that her husband, mother, and mother-in-law each has differing expectations as to how she should perform her wife's role. She finds that in adjusting to her husband's expectations she violates the expectations of significant others. It is apparent that this type of conflict is difficult to resolve, especially when each faction feels its expectations are legitimate. Sometimes it is possible to change people's expectations of the role. Sometimes one needs to perform the role in terms of his own considered definition of what is appropriate despite the demands of others. This latter action lessens one's inner conflicts but does not eliminate the external pressures.

Cautions

1. The above is a logical outline of adjustment possibilities from a particular frame of reference. It does not pretend to cover the social-psychological dynamics involved in the difficult process of attitude or behavior change. One should never presume that such adjustments are psychologically easy.

In performing a role the same response brings both reward and punishment.

I have argued that all conflict is a result of one person's behavior not meeting another's expectations or vice versa. The correction of such conflict is often more complex, for one's behavior and/or expectations may be related to one's "personality," i.e., certain temperament factors, conceptions of self, important self-other needs, and so on. The changing of one's role behavior or expectations may demand personal adjustments that are extremely difficult. One's level of maturity will also be an important factor in determining the capability of one to make adjustments.

2. The above outline does not suggest which of the types of conflict is most frequent nor which of the types of adjustment is easiest. More research is needed in the area of marital adjustment using this schema. It is, however, a commonly held position that it is easier to change one's role expectations than to change another's behavior.

3. It should be noted that there are other methods available for the *reduction* of conflict in marital situations without actually adjusting in the sense defined above; that is, the marriage partners make some alteration of norms, roles, or role expectations. This avenue generally is the alteration of the *situation* that may be fostering certain role behaviors or expectations. For example, if conflict occurs between a husband and wife because he spends too much time with a group of old cronies (his behavior thus violating her expectations), a change in residence may put so much distance between husband and friends that the situation is altered and the husband now spends time with his wife. However, since no adjustment was expected in this area, it is always possible the husband may make a new set of cronies.

The marital situation is often changed by such actions as moving, changing jobs, having a baby, or a family disaster. The altered situation may actually eliminate the point of conflict or perhaps bring about a reappraisal of role or expectations leading to adjustment as discussed herein.

It is easier to change one's role expectations than to change another's behavior.

References

Dyer, William G., and Dick Urban
 1958 "The institutionalization of equalitarian family norms." Marriage and Family Living 20 (February):53-58.

Gibb, Jack R.
 1959 Factors Producing Defensive Behavior with Groups, VI. Final Technical Report, Office of Naval Research, Nont—2285 (01).

Kelman, Herbert C.
 1956 "Three processes of acceptance of social influence: Compliance, identification, and internalization." Paper read at the meetings of the American Psychological Association, Chicago, Illinois (August 30).

Mangus, A. R.
 1957 "Family impacts on mental health." Marriage and Family Living 19 (August): 256-262.

Miller, Neal, and John Dollard
 1941 Social Learning and Imitation. New Haven: Yale University Press.

Newcomb, Theodore M.
 1950 Social Psychology. New York: Dryden Press.

Nye, Ivan, and Evelyn MacDougal
 1960 "Do families have subcultures?" Sociology and Social Research 44 (May-June):311-316.

Parsons, Talcott
 1951 The Social System. Glencoe: Free Press:38.

Verplanch, W.
 1957 "The operant, from rat to man: Some experiments in human behavior." Outside Reading in Psychology. Hartley and Hartley (eds.) New York: Cromwell Company: 127-136.

Everyone I know is a practicing motivation specialist. Motivation is an issue we face all the time no matter what our field of interest; yet the subject of motivation is so vast that it is hard to get a clear picture of all the issues involved.

The basic issue in motivation is a fairly simple one. In familiar terms, the question is: "How can Ted influence (motivate) Herb to alter his performance?" How do the Teds go about getting the Herbs to change in either (a) the amount of performance, (b) the quality of performance, or (c) the direction of performance?

Change in Amount

A common remark I hear from mothers is, "How can I get my children to do their homework, clean up their rooms, help in the house, and do the other things around here I want them to do?" Or I hear from teachers, "How can I get my students to get their work done, to write their papers, and to do more than they are doing now?" The same is true of industry and business. "How can we motivate an employee to increase the amount of his performance?"

Change in Quality

Sometimes the use of motivation is not so much "Can we get them to do more" but "Can we get them to do it better?" "My students do such a sloppy job. They get an *A* on the length of papers they turn in, but the quality is not good." "My children clean up their rooms but they are almost worse than when they started. How can we get them to do better?" So, at times, we are concerned about the quality of performance.

Change in Direction

There are times when we are concerned about a change in the direction of performance: "I wish I could get my son to spend more time on schoolwork and less time on basketball." "I wish I could get my daughter to be more interested in homemaking skills

**How can we
motivate people?**

and less interested in boys." Because we have a concern in changing the direction of performance, we turn our attention to motivation. How can we motivate people to shift direction from one focus to another, or how can we get people to improve the amount or quality of what is done? We are concerned about what we can do that will make some difference in the performance of other people.

Direct Influence Process

Compliance

One possibility in dealing with motivation is that we try *direct influence*. We try to take some kind of direct action with the person or persons upon whom we are trying to generate some change. I'd like to draw first on the work of a man by the name of Herbert Kelman (1961:57-78). He has identified three major kinds of influence processes that many of us tend to employ. He uses the terms *compliance, identification*, and *internalization*.

The compliance process is a reward or punishment process. It represents control of the reward system. You try to get people to comply with your request; and, if they do comply, you increase reward and decrease punishment. This is a very common influence strategy. "If you kids don't shape up and get your work done now, there is no TV for the next three days."

In our house when our children were younger my wife and I would have liked to have our children get up in the mornings, get dressed, clean up their rooms, finish their schoolwork, help get breakfast, help clean up the dishes, and go off to school happy and joyful. It somehow just didn't seem to work, and so we had a strategy that went something like this: my wife would say, "All right kids, come on, get breakfast." Nothing happened so she would send me downstairs. We operate from a kind of decibel theory of motivation; that is, when the voice reaches a certain pitch, "All right, move!" they really start moving. Our children have us well trained. They know that if anything is really important we, the parents, will respond. It is like the cartoon of two little brothers in their pajamas up in the bedroom playing and one little brother says, "If Daddy doesn't get up here and make us get dressed, we're going to be late for school." But when we start to yell, implicit in this is, "we had better move or they'll get mad, and that isn't very pleasant," so we move. This is the compliance process.

In schools we often make this process fairly uniform and regiment it in terms of grades. Students come in and we tell them what they have to do if they want to get an *A*. Then we tell them what can happen if they don't get their work in. This system is a fairly straightforward distribution of rewards and/or punishment. By the time students get to college they are pretty well conditioned to the process and so they comply. Motivation to them and the teacher means compliance. They are motivated to get the reward. The problem with this is that we often want people to do things for other reasons than receiving a reward. We want them to learn something because we think the material is important, not just to get a good grade. This is one of the problems in the compliance process. If we have available to us certain rewards and punishments, we can then make them available or withhold them in some kind of exchange. People know this and are motivated to change their behavior in the directions of whatever we'd like them to become in order to get the reward or to minimize punishment.

Identification

In the *process of identification* the basis of influence is in the nature of the relationship. The classic statement of identification is found in the New Testament for those of you who are theologians, where Jesus says, "If you love me, keep my commandments." (John 14:15.) This is a classic "identification statement." All of us have known or have had the experience of thinking, "George is such a wonderful person that I would do anything he would ask me to do, even if it were stupid, because I think so much of him." Or, "Mr. Johnson has always been so good and so considerate that I would be willing to do anything for him." Sometimes we find ourselves using this in a somewhat blatant kind of way. We may say something like this, "Now, I'm your mother; if you really love me, you'll remember all the good things I've done for you, and you'll do this for me." We may remember this in our own experience with our mothers and fathers. If we didn't do what they wanted us to do, it would interfere somewhat with our relationship. Now, identification overlaps into the compliance area because it can be a form of reward or punishment. The sense of identification with a person is the willingness to be influenced because of our faith and confidence in the other person and not because of the reward or punishment. If we are going to use the process of identification, we have to be sure we have the basis of a relationship at our command, otherwise our influence won't accomplish much.

Internalization

Internalization is based on the legitimacy of the argument. We are influenced by another person because the request he makes of us agrees with our own values and beliefs, and not because we are worried about rewards and punishment.

One Sunday morning I came up to get my family ready for Sunday School and my wife said, "You'll have to talk to David (our seven-year-old son)." So I asked, "What's the matter, David?" He said, "I'm not going to Sunday School." "Why don't you want to go to Sunday School, David?" He said, "I hate Jeff." (Jeff is our next boy who is three years older. They had had some kind of fight and he hates Jeff, so he's not going to Sunday School.) I wanted to see what condition would motivate David to go to Sunday School so I said, "Come on, David, I want to talk to you." We went out on the porch and I said, "David, would you go to Sunday School if I said, 'If you don't go I am really going to paddle your pants hard'? Or would you go to Sunday School if I gave you a dime? Or would you go to Sunday School if I said, 'Look, as your father, it would make me feel good and I'd appreciate it if you would go.' Would you go if it would make me feel better? Would you go to Sunday School because you really feel that is where you ought to be on Sunday, that it is the right place to learn the things you need to know, and that down deep you really know that Sunday School is the right place to be? What would get you to go to Sunday School?" David held up ten fingers. I said, "The dime, huh?" "Yeh," said David. So I said, "All right, if you go to Sunday School, I'll give you a dime." But that bothered me, because he's responding out of compliance. Motivation that comes from compliance may be a violation of our own values.

Years ago when I was an undergraduate student I heard, "There is no greater treason than to do the right thing for the wrong reasons." This is how I feel about people being motivated for certain kinds of reasons. To have my boy continue to go to Sunday School for a dime would be a kind of treason. I'm not sure that what I wanted to achieve out of this situation was just to be able to get him in Sunday School. There is another element in motivation and it is, "What is it you are attempting to accomplish in motivation?" Are you just trying to get conforming performance? If you are, then you may want to continue to use compliance. But you may never be sure that what you really want to achieve at a deeper level is going to get done. You may find that people comply just to get a reward. The issues and the research are not clear about this. A Harvard psychologist, Gordon Allport (1937) has a notion he calls *Functional Autonomy:* that is, some things we do under initial motivation later become autonomous in and of themselves. If we can get a boy to go to Sunday School for a dime over a period of time, after a while he may enjoy going to Sunday School — it will become a rewarding experience in itself. Pos-

People comply just to get a reward.

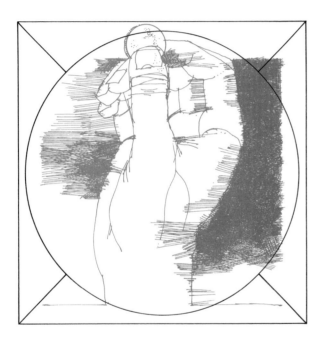

sibly, we use compliance initially as a means of building enough experience so the individual is eventually motivated by deeper values. That is what we hope, but we need to be very careful in using this strategy. If we are not careful, we often move into a bargaining situation — it will cost us fifteen cents, then twenty cents, then a quarter. We move backwards rather than getting him more and more involved in the desired experience.

I was talking with an administrator for a volunteer organization, and he told me they have different chapters coming from many areas for central meetings. When they take a standing attendance (Have people stand up from each of the chapters, count them, and give recognition to the chapter that has the greatest attendance), attendance is 30 percent higher than when they do not take a standing roll call. Now if you are a practical administrator, what is your reaction? On the one hand, you might say, "It is a lousy kind of motivation that influences people to come to a meeting just to get their chapter's attendance counted." But on the other hand, you might argue, "Isn't it better to get 30 percent more in attendance by using a compliance device, than not having them there at all?" This is a management problem with which almost everyone is confronted at some time or another.

What method of motivation are we going to use and what does it do to our own values as we try to influence people? I see my wife and I, desperate to get some help from the children, resorting to all kinds of devices. We would like to have the children help in the home because they want to keep the house lovely, but at times we find ourselves reverting to motivational strategies that are not the first on our list. What I sometimes find is that we start with compliance and move to other strategies. Before people really build much of a relationship, the initial motivation process is often direct compliance. It may be that we go through steps in motivation, going from the least desirable to the most desirable. However, I have never been able to demonstrate the sequence. I do have a feeling that we should somehow move to a higher level. I think it would be more consistent with my own values. Ultimately, it would be a more consistent system of motivation with my values to get people to respond because of the legitimacy of the argument. I think that sometimes we don't really allow this to emerge. We keep maintaining motivation at a fairly simple compliance level, the threats and reward become much more subtle, and there is a form of internalization. But the compliance is still there.

I listen to graduate students who say, "Let us work out our own design for our master's program; we are mature adults." But underneath this is, "You'd better get going and do things the way the professors want, because if you don't they can wash you up in this school. You'd better be very careful." Sometimes we think that people are operating on a higher level, but we have overlaid a heavy compliance process that is really moving people along. If we want to finally move to this different kind of motivation, we have to work on the internalization process. We have to deal with it directly and allow people the chance to operate from what they really think and believe. This is often awfully hard for people who are in authority positions to do. It is sometimes very difficult for my wife and me to allow our children the right to make their own decisions. Hopefully, we have moved them to a point where we can react as we did to our children the other night. We have three teen-agers that date, and they said, "What time do you think we ought to come in after our dates?" I said, "I think that you ought to be in about 1:00." They replied, "If we're double dating and the dance doesn't get out until 12:00 and we're driving the car, how do we get to our homes when we have to be in by 1:00?" So I said, "All right, I trust you. I think you are mature enough to make the decision to decide when you should be home." Am I really saying, "You have the right to make your decision

We have to allow people the chance to operate from what they really think and believe.

as to when you come in"? But underlying this is, "Boy, if I get up and it is late and you are not in, you and I really are going to tangle!" This is an interesting issue to look at. If we are trying to influence people to motivate themselves on the basis of the *legitimacy of the argument*, to what extent do we still have a "loaded pistol" at their heads? This constitutes direct compliance influence.

Altering the Situation

A second kind of influence process is trying to motivate people by not pushing directly at them, but by altering the situation. This is an extremely interesting strategy for a person who is trying to get another person to improve or alter his performance. Let me describe some possibilities here. In one research project, the researcher was working with a branch bank and wanted to see if he could get the girls who put out the monthly bank statements to improve their performance. On the average, these girls worked from 8:30 to 3:30 every day and were getting out 100 bank statements a day. They were concerned with improving the *amount* of performance. The practical question was, how could they go about trying to get the girls to produce more bank statements? What are some possible strategies? (1) If they get over 100 done, pay them extra money — this is compliance, but bank officials didn't want to do that. (2) Isolate them so that they couldn't waste their time. This would be altering the situation. The officials didn't want to do that either. What else? Finally they followed this procedure. Company officials told the girls, "As soon as you get 150 bank statements done, you can go home." On the average, the girls were able to finish and go home at 1:00 p.m. For these girls, time was a much more important factor than other rewards, but to change this factor meant also altering the nature of the workday. The situation of the workday hours had to be redefined. Sometimes we don't pick up ways of altering the situation. We get so involved in attempts at direct influence through what we say, or how we can push, that we don't think of other possibilities of restructuring the situation. The bank officials looked at the quality of the girls' work and found no drop-off even with the increased output. The quality was every bit as good as it was before. What they didn't find out, incidentally, was that letting some people go home at 1:00 affected the other people in the system who did not go home early. It is like letting one child stay up and watch television and making the other stay in the bedroom and do his work. There are repercussions in the system. One part of the system has one type of motivation condition and another has a different condition; this can lead to disruptions in the system.

I want to mention the work of a theorist by the name of Frederick Herzberg (1966). He developed a theory of motivation which I wish to examine at this point. Herzberg says that in any organizational situation there are two sets of factors: one creates satisfaction or dissatisfaction and one creates motivation. The person who is trying to improve motivation often starts by working on the satisfiers in the situation and neglects the motivation factors. Herzberg asked people what it is that makes them unhappy or dissatisfied in their work. They gave such answers as, "We don't have a good relationship with our boss, we don't like the people we are working with, the work is dirty, we don't like our salary," and so on. If the situation is improved and the people are given good working conditions, good supervision, good salaries, and pleasant working relationships, feelings of satisfaction result. Herzberg says making people satisfied does not motivate people. They feel better about the working conditions, but they don't work harder, or they don't work with better quality or change their directions.

A major problem in organizations is presented by people who manage—the parents, teachers, and administrators. They try to alter the situation by manipulating the satisfiers. However, Herzberg says

A major problem in organization is presented by people who manage — the parents, teachers, and administrators.

that what motivates people is to be given a job that is challenging, rewarding, and leads to advancement and growth. Motivation lies in the nature of the work they have to do. If we assign people meaningless, routine, mundane work and we want them to do more of it, it is hard to provide motivation. Herzberg makes a strong case for what he calls *job enrichment*. Many organizations are attempting to enrich the job so that people are motivated because the work itself is more challenging and rewarding.

Some of the things Herzberg has done with organizations have been interesting. Instead of having workers just do one kind of task he gives a group of workers the responsibility for an entire activity. They have to organize, plan, distribute, and so forth. Their motivation increases because they now have something that is challenging. Sometimes our strategy when something isn't done very well is to break down this meaningless something into even smaller bits so it will be easier. But this doesn't motivate. The issue Herzberg is raising is that if we can increase the complexity, the challenge, the responsibility, and the recognition that a person gets in doing something, only then do we deal with motivation. If we are going to alter the situation, we should think about enriching the situation for people.

Motivation and Needs

Maslow (1943:370-396) says that all of us have basic kinds of needs: physiological, safety, social, ego, and what he calls self-actualization. These needs are in a hierarchy from lower needs — physiological — to the highest and most complex — self-actualization. Argyris (1957) says that what happens in most organizations is that conditions are established that are geared at satisfying the lower-level needs, and the higher needs of people go begging.

Some people never have a chance to fulfill their higher needs, such as, relating to other people, having satisfying, meaningful contact with others, having a sense of inclusion and affection and response. We never allow these needs to be satisfied because we deal situationally with needs at the lowest level possible. Maslow says that a satisfied need is not a motivator. When we are in the process of building or buying a new home, we look at everyone's house. When it is finally built or bought, we don't look at houses with the same sense of urgency. The need is met and it is no longer a motivator.

In our motivation system, we often create conditions that satisfy one level and never allow people to move on up. This is what Herzberg (1966) is also saying. We create work that does not allow people to satisfy ego needs, to feel that "I'm doing something worthwhile" or that "I have the esteem of people." We do not create conditions wherein people achieve the best that is possible for them to achieve (self-actualization).

My guess is that what children are asked to do is at a very simple level; there is not much chance for them to achieve any kind of result in higher needs areas. We don't look at how we can alter that situation, how we can allow people a greater investment of themselves so that they can get some growth or challenge out of it. In a rural society a boy has to work because he knows the family depends on the crops. His work is quite a different situation from trying to get a boy in the urban family to be motivated to make his bed or take out the garbage. These tasks do not allow him to actualize anything. Parents need to find ways for children to develop. In all cases job enrichment is important.

Motivation through Objectives

There is a program called *management by objectives* or *teaching by objectives*. The notion here is, instead of telling students, "If you do this, you are going to get an *A* or *B* or *C*," that we allow people to set their own goals and objectives and involve them in making decisions. If we let students participate in the process of goal setting, planning, and decision making, we find there is an improvement in motiva-

tion. People are willing to work harder with greater quality or in different directions when they have a chance to influence the situation themselves.

Feedback

Another possibility in motivation is to increase the information or data factor. McClelland (1962:99-112) has done extensive work on achievement motivation. One of the things we know about people who have high achievement motivation is that it makes a real difference in their performance if they get immediate, accurate feedback on how they are doing. However, the type of feedback is important, for people respond defensively and negatively to distorted, evaluative, or judgmental feedback.

Competition

Another manner for altering situations is to introduce competition. Competition works well in certain situations. In our culture we are competitively oriented—we like to win. We like challenge. We can sometimes get people to do things if we can say, "Look, that's what people in the other department are doing; we can do better than that."

However, I saw some dangerous overtones from competition among my own children when they were young. We wanted to get them dressed and fed in the morning, and they wanted to sit around and play in or with the food and not get dressed. So we set up a very simple system. "All right, let's see who can get dressed first; let's see who can get the food down. Come on. Hurray for Mike, he won!" We began to notice a lot of negative effects between the two older boys. They didn't like each other; they developed resentments. We were getting the food down and the clothes on, but we were noticing side effects that we didn't like.

I hear example after example given of people who have used competition as a way of getting people to perform. To achieve and win is a tremendous motivating force. Boys in athletics compete in teams. They

98

spend tremendous time and energy in competing. I wonder what happens to those who lose. This is a side effect. I remember reading *Peanuts* one time: Schultz's Charlie Brown was telling Linus about his dream. "Boy, I had the greatest dream about a big football game at the homecoming. The home team was behind, six to nothing, and at the last minute the home team threw a long pass, scored a touchdown, and kicked the extra point. Just as the game ended, they won, seven to six, and the crowd went wild." And Linus said, "I wonder how the other team felt."

In conclusion, in trying to motivate another person, here are some of the strategies that are open: direct influence, altering the situation in some way, getting more feedback, or using competition. Each strategy requires an understanding of self, the people involved, the nature of the system, and the goals one is trying to achieve. Motivation is complex, but with more insight we might also be more successful.

References

Allport, Gordon W.
1937   Personality: A Psychological Interpretation. New York: Henry Holt & Co.

Argyris, Chris
1957   Personality and Organization. New York: Harper & Row, Publishers.

Herzberg, Frederick
1966   Work and the Nature of Man. Cleveland: World Publishing Co.

Kelman, Herbert C.
1961   "Process of opinion change." Public Opinion Quarterly XXV (Spring): 57-78.

McClelland, David
1962   "Business drive and national achievement." Harvard Business Review (July-August): 99-112.

Maslow, Abraham
1943   "A theory of human motivation." Psychology Review 50:370-396.

2
Barriers
to Change

Change is not easy and anyone who has adopted New Year's resolutions and has seen them slowly slip away knows of the difficulties. This section points out some of the forces that intrude themselves into situations and make change difficult. The chapter on manipulation points out that some people can pretend at change. They may try to alter some external behavior but inside they are calculating how to get more what they want. Such action is a violation of the idea of congruence. Manipulative behavior is resented; and, if people are resentful, they often resist the changes the manipulator is trying to instigate.

Sometimes when a person makes a change it is greeted with acceptance by some but with resistance by others. Such is the basis of internal role conflict. Sometimes we change to meet the expectations of some persons but we violate the expectations of others. Since change may not be uniformly accepted by everyone, the change attempt may put the person into deep conflict, a condition that may result in retreat from change, unless one learns to cope with it well.

Finally, it is also a common experience that when one wants to change there are rules, regulations, norms, and practices that have been built into the fabric of a system that make change difficult if not impossible. Certain cultural barriers block attempts to do things differently or better, and one needs to plan change carefully to take such barriers into account.

Manipulation*

In this age of enlightened management it may well be that certain rather autocratic executives are beginning to experience an identity crisis following a training group experience, managerial training program, or the acquisition of an advanced degree in administration. Since the arrival of McGregor's *Human Side of Enterprise* (1960) more than a decade ago, few MBA graduates are not thoroughly knowledgeable with Theory X and Theory Y, assumptions about human behavior in the industrial world. Having been exposed to modern theories of management, the autocratic administrator becomes well aware of the kind of executive he *should* be. This "should be" image, however, may be very incongruent with his "want to be" image as the man who runs a very tight, nononsense organization.

He is thus faced with a dilemma regarding the degree to which he should allow his subordinates to participate in managerial decisions. He is faced, on the one hand, with a desire to allow his underlings to become self-actualized in their respective organizational roles through exercising their own initiative and creative skills in making decisions and implementing them. On the other hand, he is confronted by the horrible thought that his subordinates might possibly make a wrong decision if left to their own devices.

Tannenbaum and Schmidt (1958:95-101) have proposed a very useful model of participatory management which includes varying degrees of group involvement on a continuum ranging from very little to almost total group participation:

1. Manager makes decision and announces it.
2. Manager "sells" decision.
3. Manager presents ideas and invites questions.
4. Manager presents tentative decision.
5. Manager presents problem, gets suggestions, makes decision.
6. Manager defines limits; asks group to make decision.

---

*William G. Dyer and Spencer J. Condie.

7. Manager permits subordinates to function within limits defined by superior.

For some leaders, managers or executives, each of the above points on the continuum might represent alternative leadership *styles* or behavioral patterns congruent with their own personality and individual needs. For other individuals in superordinate positions, the continuum may represent alternative leadership *strategies*, i.e., ways of getting people to do what you want them to do.

The Illusionary Democratic Leader

An all too frequent phenomenon is the leader who wishes to appear to have adopted a number 6 or 7 style in the Tannenbaum-Schmidt model but instead uses this style as a manipulative strategy, while in reality he is operating at the number 1 level of decision-making participation. We shall refer to such a strategy as *illusionary democratic leadership*. In such a case the leader may present the parameters of a given problem and suggest some alternative solutions to the problem; the final solution of which is supposedly derived through group participation. However, in most cases the illusionary democratic leader will already have implemented the decision which eludes the preview of the unknowingly retroactive group discussion.

Benevolent Autocrat

One of the earliest styles identified as a manipulative strategy is the *benevolent autocrat* (Bradford and Lippitt, 1945). This leader disguises his authoritarian bent in the form of the wise, kindly father who is only doing what he must do for "your good." Subordinates are thought of, and treated, as little children who are not yet mature enough to function independently and who therefore must be guided, directed, and protected from their own shortcomings.

The benevolent autocrat can be of two types: the autocratic leader who honestly believes that he is like a father to his subordinates and believes that his

The wise, kindly father does what he must do for "your own good."

wisdom and experience entitle him to make decisions for others; the other type is the person who adopts the paternalistic stance because it seems to put him out of reach of any adverse reaction. After all, who can attack daddy! This person assumes the kindly, benevolent pose but doesn't feel that way toward others. He finds it a more comfortable posture than taking the gloves off and demanding obedience and conformity.

The Pseudofamily

Gouldner (1950:644-659) has delineated a managerial strategy which centers around a series of actions taken on the part of the leader designed to create within the worker the feeling that he is part of a close-knit "family" unit and that the subordinate owes it to the unit to work hard in achieving organizational goals. He refers to this manipulative group cohesiveness as a "pseudo-*Gemeinschaft*" in that the leader is not genuinely concerned with building group integration, but deliberately wants to create a group identity; so he can use the group as a basis of influence and coercion.

In such a pseudo-*Gemeinschaft* the manager creates a false group feeling by (1) talking very personally to the workers in order to create the impression that they are all very close in their relationship; (2) engaging in personal favors which obligate his subordinates to do his bidding; (3) shifting members who resist his influence out of the group in a nonobvious way; (4) spending an inordinate amount of time being "around" people, while subtly conveying his omnipresence; (5) instituting a system of reports under the guise of just wanting to know what is going on; and (6) keeping everyone busy even if the work isn't relevant or important.

Managerial Facade

A close relative to the above manager is the leader who adopts the Blake-Mouton *managerial facade* (1964:192-212). From a distrust of group decision-making ability the managerial facade strategist may "feel out positions and achieve commitment from those concerned, prior to assembling them." By composing a decision-making group exclusively of one's allies, the manager is able to present the facade of allowing extensive participation and group involvement when, in fact, the outcome of such a group discussion was ensured prior to the group's inception.

The Phony Proposer

A variation on this same theme is the *phony proposer*, a person identified in research by Lawrence (1954). He is another under-the-skin autocrat who for some reason feels he must at least go through the motions of participatory management. His strategy is to present his own ideas to the group in the form of a proposal with a very obvious flaw in it. He supposes that as the group dutifully picks out the flaw and meticulously perfects the proposal they will achieve a sense of group-fulfillment in achieving a decision together. Akin to this form of illusionary democracy is the person who offers two proposals, both of his own choosing, but asks the group to decide on the final outcome. The catch is that one proposal is infinitely superior to the other, so that participation in the final decision can hardly be equated with involvement.

The Public Praiser

A style of manipulation that has been observed but not studied in depth is seen in the person who runs his operation his way by direct authority and control, but whenever he discusses his operation for public consumption via newspapers, radio, or television, he expresses credit to "his wonderful team of cooperative assistants." As in all of the manipulative strategies, this form is designed to protect the autocrat from attack and criticism from others. If one has publicly declared that the results of the enterprise were from a team effort and credit and praise are given to others, what ungrateful person would then

criticize the process. Reports from subordinates caught in situations with the public praiser indicate the ambivalence they feel toward him. They resent his autocratic methods but appreciate the public recognition. They also recognize that the public statements do not agree with the facts as they have experienced them, but, since the publicity reflects favorably on them, it has some pleasing aspects.

The Impotent Committee

Another manipulative strategy is to create the impression that others are going to be involved in the planning or decision-making process by assigning work out to a committee. Some autocrats have all members of the organization on at least one committee, giving the false feeling that everyone will share in the developments of the organization. However, the leader so manipulates the use of the committee that the committee actions are never really implemented or have a chance to have impact.

There are a number of devices that can be used to make a committee impotent:

1. Committee reports must be first cleared through an "executive committee" which is controlled by the boss, and it is this executive group that has final authority.

2. The committee is asked to be a recommending body only and then the votes are loaded to come out the way the leader wants.

3. Committees are not given adequate time to meet, resulting in inadequate work; so decisions must be made on a "crisis" basis with the excuse that "We just can't wait on the committee as much as we would like to."

4. Committee assignments are made so the critical areas are not turned over to a committee; the boss retains them himself and keeps committees involved in noncritical matters. It is also possible for the boss to place himself along with certain trusted lieutenants on the really critical committees so he can control the proposals that result.

Consequences of Manipulative Strategies

Observation and research have been done on the effects of manipulative strategies on peers and subordinates. More research is needed. However, it appears that one of the major consequences is the pushing of resistance to the manipulative leader down to a very covert, subtle level. Since there is the guise of participation and democracy, the person being manipulated feels guilty and off-balance if he confronts the leader. He knows that if he cites examples of manipulation the leader can cite examples of his apparent involvement of others. Thus the confrontation is "my opinion against yours," and the confronter fears that he will appear as a sorehead, an ingrate, or a power and status seeker. With resistance and negative reaction at an undercover level, it is difficult to deal with the negative effects of the leader. It often takes a skillful outsider to uncover the leadership style and its eroding effects.

In recent years considerable research has been directed toward that ancient breed of manipulators, the *Machiavellians* (Christie, 1970:82-86). As opposed to the autocratic leader who apparently has certain needs to dominate, the Machiavellian is an unabashed manipulator of superb expertise. The honest autocrat will read this paper and admit it. He then may or may not alter his managerial style. The true Machiavellian, however, will read this article and chuckle to himself.

The true Machiavellian will read this article and chuckle to himself.

Conclusion

Regardless of one's personal needs or desires, if a leader cannot trust his subordinates with open participation in administrative decisions, he should at least spare them from the hypocrisy of illusionary democracy. Perhaps the autocratic executive must ease into a freer managerial style by allowing decisions of lesser import to be made by subordinates and then gradually delegating more and more authority to them. Upon evaluating the quality of their decisions, and after observing the valuable error-detection mechanism of group discussion, the executive may become aware of the tremendous potential creativity which he has unlocked in his underlings and himself as well.

References

Blake, Robert R., and Jane S. Mouton
    1964   The Managerial Grid. Houston: Gulf Publishing Company: 192-211.

Bradford, Leland P., and Ronald Lippitt
    1945   "Building a democratic work group." Personnel 22(November): 143-144.

Christie, Richard
    1970   "The Machiavellians among us." Psychology Today (November): 82-86.

Gouldner, Alvin W. (ed.)
    1950   Studies in Leadership: Leadership and Democratic Action. New York: Harper & Row Publishers: 644-659.

Lawrence, Paul
    1954   "How to deal with resistance to change." Harvard Business Review (May-June): 56.

McGregor, Douglas
    1960   The Human Side of Enterprise. New York: McGraw-Hill.

Tannenbaum, Robert T., and Warren H. Schmidt
    1958   "How to choose a leadership pattern." Harvard Business Review (March-April): 95-101.

One of the common clichés of our time is "we live in a complex society." This phrase is used in a variety of contexts, but it often refers to conditions that bewilder and confuse, and one explains his confusion and dilemma by saying, philosophically, that "we live in a complex society." Others nod wisely and sympathetically in agreement.

Like many clichés, the theme is essentially correct, but it offers no real insight. Recent explorations in theory and research in the behavioral sciences, especially role theory, offer some real insights into conditions that produce the almost helpless explanation, "we live in a complex society."

Conflict

Roles

Nearly all persons observe that as they move from one situation or set of relationships to another their behavior changes. One does not behave the same way in church as he does at work, at home, at a party, or at a lodge meeting. Each situation demands some different responses which most people assume. In social science parlance each different set of responses is a *role* — that behavior which is expected in a given situation. Complexity and confusion come as people multiply the number of roles impinging upon them without realizing the forces at work.

First, it is important to note that in each situation where one assumes a role, others involved in the situation have at their disposal the power to reward or punish each person to the degree he fulfills or fails to fulfill his role obligations. If a young lady in her daughter role does not keep her room clean (one part of the role obligation), then her parents may apply certain punishments by reducing her allowance, scolding her, or denying other benefits.

Second, it should be recognized that most people internalize the demands of the role; that is, the expected role behavior becomes a part of the need system of the individual. In order to maintain his self-respect, his respect from others, his feelings of adequacy and self-worth, the individual needs to

The expected
role behavior
becomes a part
of the need system
of the individual.

perform those roles he has accepted. If a person who has internalized a role does not conform to the demands of the role, he is afflicted with self-punishment — feelings of guilt or self-effacement — even though there is no other person present to apply an external punishment. Thus a boy who drinks with the gang and wins their approval may suffer pangs of guilt knowing this violates the demands of his role as a church member.

Punishment or reward, then, may stem from other persons or from within the person himself. People are generally very sensitive to these reactions and try consciously or unconsciously to maintain themselves in an overall condition where there is a maximum amount of reward and a minimum of punishment. One must recognize, of course, that individuals differ in their definitions of reward and punishment.

Problems and conflict arise when people get caught in situations where, by performing a role, the same response brings *both* reward and punishment. This is the basis of role conflict. Role conflict can be divided into two general classes: conflict of multiple roles and conflict internal to a role. These can, in turn, be subdivided. Conflicts between roles can be a conflict of norms or a conflict of time. Conflict within a role can be conflict of time, of needed ability, or of expectations.

Multiple Roles

One of the most common sources of serious conflict lies in the disparity between the demands of two roles one person is expected to take. Teen-agers often find that their role in their peer group demands different behavior from their role in the home or their role as church members. To steal hub caps may elicit the approval of the gang as being an appropriate peer group response, but it brings swift disapproval from the parent or the minister.

Essentially this indicates a conflict of group norms from which the roles are derived. The norms of group A may demand certain actions, while the norms of group B may pressure for behavior which is diametrically opposed to that of group A. This involves not only conflicting pressures from others, but personal conflicts to the individual who may be personally oriented to both sets of norms. Thus he has guilt feelings when he behaves one way even if persons in the other group do not know of his "deviant" behavior.

This type of conflict is found among many people: businessmen who are caught between accepted business practices of the cutthroat nature and Christian ethics suggesting that you "love your neighbor as yourself"; students who are pressured by classmates to cheat, in conflict with home and church norms; or members of a Republican family who belong to a Democratic social group.

How do people handle this type of role conflict? Obviously everyone in this conflict of multiple roles does not crack-up under the strain. There are a number of psychologically protective devices that are used. Some use various defense mechanisms such as rationalization or repression. Others compartmentalize; that is, they put each role in a separate mental compartment and refuse to see any conflict. Some fortunate few are able to make a decision to withdraw from one of the conflict groups in light of some priority of values. Many continue to operate within a system of stress, anxiety, pressure, and guilt feelings, being unable to eliminate either of the conflicting roles.

Time conflict is another type of multiple-role conflict. This conflict is the common phenomenon wherein a person assumes so many roles in so many groups that he cannot possibly fulfill all of the obligations involved. As a result each group is applying pressures to get the person to involve himself in its activity. Thus a person in this situation may receive rewards from one group for spending his time on that group's program, but he may also receive negative pressures from another group for not having spent time with them. The classic example is the man who moves ahead professionally but receives negative reactions from his family for not spending more time with them.

In this type of conflict a person is commonly under a constant feeling of pressure for the decision to perform one of the many roles demanding attention. Knowing this, each group tries to apply the maximum amount of pressure, vying for the participation of this overloaded person. Fortunate is the person who can evaluate his many roles and eliminate or redefine some roles to reduce the conflict and tension level.

Conflict Internal to a Role

Conflicts also occur within a single role, and the *time factor* again is involved. This is closely tied with the matter of multiple group membership, for a person may accept a role and find that he really does not have time to meet the demands of the role; yet he does not know how to get out of the role obligation.

Secondly, there is the matter of *necessary ability*. In this case a person may accept a role for which he has time, and for which there is no conflict with any other role, but he discovers that the role demands actions which he feels he does not have the ability to fulfill. A person who is shy and retiring may for various reasons accept a role as a fund raiser in an organization and is then terrified at the prospects of visiting people and asking them for money. The role hangs over his head like an awesome burden, and he often thinks of all kinds of reasons why he doesn't have time to carry out the assignment, or else he completes the task, detesting it all the time and refusing to do anything in the organization again.

From this, one would naturally assume that the wisest course would be to match role demands with skills and ability. This is easier said than done. On the one hand it is possible that a person may have the latent ability and could grow with the job even though he feels inadequate. On the other hand a person may be overconfident and willing to accept,

The role hangs over his head like an awesome burden.

but not be competent in actual performance.

The acceptance of a role for which a person feels he does not have the necessary ability results in receiving certain rewards from the group, but accompanying it are feelings of self-torture and pressures which are very real and very painful.

Expectations Influence Role Taking

Finally one needs to examine the situation where a person finds himself in conflict because of different people having differing *expectations* as to how his role should be carried out. A teacher may find that some parents expect her to be a strict disciplinarian while others feel she should be very permissive and accepting. By performing the role one way she receives the approval of one set of parents but the angry reactions of the other. A reversal of behavior does not remove her from the conflict. This type of conflict is even more frustrating when people do not define their expectations of the role, and the person is the recipient of negative reactions without knowing what he has done to elicit this response. This conflict is a constant source of difficulty for the newly married. The husband may define his role one way. His wife expects quite different things from him. Yet neither communicates his expectations to the other. Thus the husband, by fulfilling his own definition of the role, violates the expectations of his wife and is subjected to a bewildering series of tears, pouts, and rebuffs. People often are unable to communicate openly and honestly their expectations to each other and make adjustments to each other via the painful trial-and-error method.

It is obviously impossible to meet everyone's expectations in those cases where one's role is accompanied by several conflicting expectations. The old tale of the couple and the donkey illustrates the point graphically. In trying to meet everyone's expectations, the couple wound up carrying the donkey which is, of course, a ridiculous adjustment to the situation. It is also apparent that this type of conflict is difficult to resolve, especially when each faction feels its expectations are legitimate. Sometimes it is possible to change people's expectations of the role. Sometimes one needs to perform the role in terms of his own considered definition of what is appropriate despite the demands of others. This latter action lessens one's inner conflicts but does not eliminate the external pressures.

If we put together all of the possible types of role conflict situations mentioned above, it becomes apparent that this is indeed a "very complex society." Imagine the person who has too many roles, some of which represent opposing group norms, some of which demand actions for which he has inadequate skills, and some of which represent responses to conflicting expectations. In each case others are applying constant pressures to this person, trying to get him to fulfill the role as the organization defines it, and at the same time the person himself is suffering from feelings of inadequacy and guilt. With this insight the cliché is no longer an insipid comment but a serious reality of today.

The movement emphasizing group-centered leadership is finding popular acceptance in education, industry, and religious circles. The trend still meets resistance from some persons or groups whose orientation to certain other cultural trends causes them to view with hostility and suspicion this move toward democratic action.

Basic to the "group dynamics" approach to leadership is the idea that all group members should work together on the problem at hand and have a share in the decision-making process. Shared action requires that each member of the group be considered as individually important. His ideas and contributions must be seen as important to the overall functioning of the group. It is apparent that this process increases the democratic nature of group action, for in a democracy each person is considered equal and each person's ideas are equated with everyone else's.

This idea of democratic procedure has long and deep roots in American culture. Americans are fond of quoting from the Declaration of Independence that "all men are created equal." However there are other cultural roots, just as deep and strong, that create barriers to pure democratic action.

This discussion points out some of these resistant factors so that they may more intelligently be understood and handled. It should be noted that different groups, sections of the country, and social strata exhibit these characteristics in differing degrees. Thus the barriers to democratic action and the method of handling the barriers will change as one shifts from place to place.

Barrier One: Sex Roles

While the status of women has been raised considerably in the United States in the past forty years, there is still a strong patriarchal tradition existing in many parts of the country. This tradition emphasizes the "natural" superiority of the male with his right to

*Revised. Reprinted by special permission from Adult Leadership, "Cultural barriers to leadership," William G. Dyer (January 1959).

ultimate powers in decision making. Women as well as men operate in this tradition. Many women in mixed groups feel it is the natural prerogative of the man to assume authority and make final decisions. In many groups this leads to a domination of the group by men. There are often feelings of resentment on the part of some men, and women too, when some women voice their ideas with vigor and expect equal opportunities in group activities.

Accompanying this idea of traditional male authority is the feeling held by many that there are certain areas held to be the domain of the male (this may also operate in reverse fashion). Some men will operate in democratic fashion with women in some areas, but when it comes to other subjects — often politics, sports, sex, money matters — these are considered "man's talk." A woman, no matter how competent, has difficulty making a contribution.

Barrier Two: Prestige

It appears to be a rather natural thing to accord more prestige, deference, and authority to those persons who have acquired more of certain items that are held in esteem in our culture. We tend to look up to those persons who have greater experience, age, education, money, and social position. Not only do many people who are lacking in these areas feel inadequate to talk on an equal basis with the more favorably endowed, but they also feel that these people have a natural right to occupy positions of dominance. They may feel it presumptuous of themselves to question, criticize, or comment. Then, too, many of these higher status people feel they should be accorded more prestige and authority.

Some people will be able to make a superior contribution in certain areas because of a higher degree of competence. However, one person is seldom, if ever, superior in all areas, and there is no reason why he should be constantly accorded or should assume positions of authority. We often find people who make a claim to positions of dominance because of greater age, and our cultural patterns support this idea of respect and deference both to parents and all older people.

When people have wealth or social position, they are often accorded higher status than is warranted by their objectively considered competency, knowledge, or skills. These feelings of superiority or inferiority are real blocks to effective democratic action.

Barrier Three: Formal Status

Closely allied to barrier two is the matter of a formal status hierarchy found in many organizations. Many of them have a division of labor and authority ranked very precisely in terms of offices ranging from president on down to supervisors, foremen, and finally workers or lay members. Such an organization is found in most businesses, schools, churches, and government agencies.

When people of varying ranks get together, those in the lower positions often feel very reluctant to participate as equals. A second lieutenant does not easily offer criticism of the policies of the base commander, nor does a file clerk or bank teller feel free to openly and equally discuss his views of the company with the president. The feeling that one's job may be in jeopardy if he violates the rules or expectations of the higher status person reduces many people to the role of "yes-men." The reverse also occurs — a higher status person may resent the equal participation of a lower ranking person. He might perceive this participation as a threat to his own position or feel that those in authority over him disapprove of such action.

Barrier Four: Formal Leadership

A most common barrier to equality of group action is the persistent cultural norm concerning the necessity and desirability of every group's having a formal leader. Even in groups where the first three barriers may not be present — a group of the same sex, equal prestige, and organizational status — a common procedure is to elect one person the formal leader and consciously or unconsciously endow him with greater powers than the rest.

This should not be confused with the desirability of having a formal leader who performs certain useful functions for the group such as calling the meeting to order, setting the agenda, and operating as a mediator for discussion. What is meant here is the too often accepted assumption by both the group members and the formally appointed leader that once a person has been appointed a formal leader, he has greater insights, abilities, powers of discernment and analysis, and greater wisdom than the other members.

In such cases the formal leader tends to dominate the meeting, initiate more action, and is looked upon as being the final authority. In reality the group as a whole probably possesses all of these qualities to a greater degree than does the one leader.

Barrier Five: Prejudice

One of the most prevalent of the resistant forces to democratic action is the matter of prejudice. Our culture helps maintain and perpetuate prejudice through the establishing of certain discriminatory practices which are handed down from parent to child as a part of his cultural inheritance.

Prejudice is a strong, persistent, emotional attitude toward any object. We think most often in terms of racial or religious prejudice, but one may have feelings of prejudice against other persons because of such factors as politics, occupation, family background, or place of origin. These feelings of prejudice constantly interfere with productive, effective group action. Good communication is interrupted in the group as persons listen and respond through their screen of prejudice. Often people fail to listen to or immediately reject the ideas of a person because of *who* the person is rather than *what* the person says.

Prejudice may result in discrimination in the group as persons are left off committees, assigned to routine or drudgery tasks, not allowed to assume positions of

The formal leader tends to dominate the meeting.

responsibility, or even completely ignored. Thus they are unable to enrich the group with their personal resources.

Through the years it has become culturally acceptable to react in prejudiced ways toward certain kinds of people, particularly those in minority groups. As a result, persons who interrupt the group with acts of prejudice may find the weight of cultural practice in their favor. Those who may object to their behavior often allow it to persist because "everyone does it" or "that's the way lots of people feel." Thereby they contribute to the continuation of prejudice and discrimination.

Overcoming the Barriers

One might well ask here — what can be done to eliminate or diminish these barriers in our group? The solutions are more easily listed than accomplished. It should be remembered that people hold the above attitudes as a result of early and persistent cultural conditioning. And, while one group may wish to change attitudes, there are other groups to which these people belong that foster and encourage barrier attitudes. One should not expect to effect immediate change, for attitudes change slowly at best. However, we might well remember the following suggestions:

1. *Examine our own behavior.* Do we create barriers to democratic action in our group because we persist in some of the practices listed above? The two areas of change are change in one's self and change in others. Awareness that one holds certain attitudes is the first step in changing attitudes.

2. *Discuss these barriers openly and frankly in the group.* This, of course, assumes that the emotional climate of the group is such that these matters may be freely and openly discussed without creating more problems than are solved. If, however, the group as a whole recognizes the problem then each person may help the others in the group.

3. *Give warm acceptance to the person who holds*

barrier attitudes. Attitude change is most effectively produced by one's friends in warm, primary-type relationships. Rejection of the person is not the answer. Rejection not only prohibits the rejected one from making a contribution to the group but often reinforces the very attitudes we wish to change.

4. *Adopt the idea of trying out new things.* It is easier to change if we have had a good experience in the new procedure or behavior pattern we are considering adopting. If any of the above barriers exist in your group, consciously try out the reverse procedure, e.g., let the women present the program on politics; assign an important task to the lowest status person; put a subordinate at the head of a committee composed of his superiors; try operating without a formal leader. These new experiences carried out in an atmosphere of friendliness and acceptance can help us get new perspectives.

5. *Have periodic sessions of evaluation and analysis of the group.* We need to constantly assess in order to be sure that new barriers are not being introduced into our group.

Rejection of the person is not the answer.

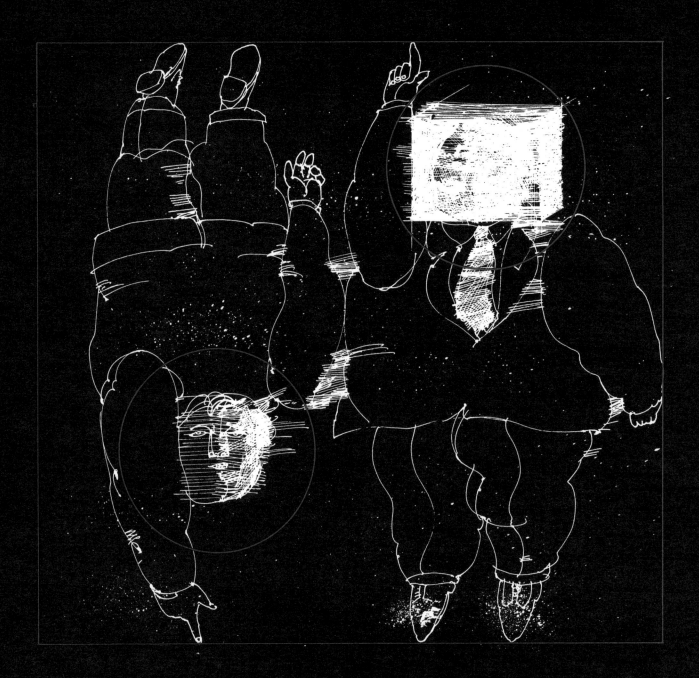

3
Change Directions: The Professional Challenge

Those whose careers center around the problem of change face a many-faceted world. At times change agents may help others achieve a change that results in a burst of improvement and carries with it accolades for the change agent; yet at other times change attempts go sour and the reaction is something like "What are we payin' him for?"

Certain methods open to the change agent include data gathering and feedback, interviewing, training, consulting, diagnosing a system and sharing the diagnosis, and working directly with an individual, a a group, or a total organization. Writings in this section cover a wide range of change agent interventions.

Any change agent must be aware of how he enters into a relationship with a client, whether it be a single person, a group, or a larger system. In any event he must build a relationship between himself and his client. This process is examined as well as the general process of consulting with a system. A special situation for many is the family, thus the role of the change agent in the family is the concern of one chapter.

The group trainer or facilitator is one type of change agent and the chapter on groups looks at the kinds of behaviors open to the group trainer that seem to facilitate growth of those in the group.

Sometimes the work of the change agent involves a total organization or system. He then needs a framework for understanding that system so he can plan a change program that will have the maximum possible success. A change program cannot be much better than the diagnosis upon which the program rests. The chapter on systems outlines a framework for diagnosing any system.

Finally there is a chapter describing one change strategy for achieving organization change. Based on a program developed at RCA, the elements in this change program combine a laboratory group training approach with the use of internal organization change agents. This is a rather sophisticated change design that might be applicable to other larger systems or to smaller systems with some modifications.

What Is Training?

Training as presently used refers to any type of education program that leads to an improvement of performance by a person or persons engaged in an ongoing activity. Underlying the idea of training is the assumption that people can change behavior and that for various reasons (to be discussed) people should engage in activities that will lead to an improvement of performance.

Improvement is generally seen as behavior or performance that is more efficient — gets more output with less expenditure of resources, or more effective — that is the person behaves qualitatively in such a way that goals are achieved with "better" (qualitatively) results. In the case of managers, training in the first sense might make the manager more efficient — that is, he might be taught how to organize his time in such a way that he accomplishes the same amount of work in less time. Or he might become more effective — that is, we might teach the manager how to handle counseling problems in such a way that people feel better about being helped after seeing the manager.

When Should We Train People?

This is an important question and should be thought about seriously. We have a general cultural value which says that everyone can improve himself; no one is perfect. This suggests that everyone could, with benefit, go through some training concerning every facet of his total life since everyone can always improve himself. This orientation taken to its absurd limits would finally result in everyone spending all of his time in some type of "training." This is the important question: Is there some level of performance (either a minimum level or an optimum level) that people should achieve; and, if they have not reached this level, then should some type of training be instigated? Usually organizations have not thought through what levels or limits should be

128

reached through training. But since we believe in improvement, all kinds of training programs are constantly being initiated with the hopes that they will do some good. This also suggests that most training programs have little or no evaluation attached to them to determine if the training has accomplished its proposed goals.

1. However, if performance levels have been established and if people have not achieved these levels, then it would seem that training of some type would be appropriate.

2. Training is also seen as necessary as a means of improving performance when a person is inexperienced in the role or job demands. Thus a person new to a position often goes through a training program as the educative means of preparing him to perform his job at the required level.

When Should We Not Train People?

Despite the cultural value that anyone can improve, there are probably times when training should not be utilized.

1. The time taken for the training program would not be worth the benefits that would accrue.

2. The beneficial results of the training program are questionable.

3. The training program would result in behavior change that really is not functional.

4. More effective results can be achieved by simpler methods (less time consuming, less costly).

In a managers' program, we might engage in a program to train all managers in the art of counseling, but it might be simpler to redefine the managers' job as that of referring people with counseling problems to a trained professional. Of course, there would have to be a provision for trained counselors on an organizational basis.

Types of Training Programs

In the attempts to bring about an improvement of performance, a great many actions are taken. Some

There are probably times when training should not be utilized.

Structured Learning Programs

The hope here is that people will read or listen to material describing new ways of behaving; they then will understand it well enough and will be sufficiently motivated that they will begin to try out the new behaviors on their own. The problems here are those of communication, understanding, and motivation. It is hard to determine if people reading or hearing material really understand it the way the author intended. Then it is even more difficult to know if the person being exposed to the material is capable of putting into behavior the kind of performance the author intended.

This kind of program is weak by itself. It needs other actions to help understand what is presented and to help people begin to put the material into action.

Training Meetings, Programs, Conferences

There are a wide variety of training programs. The poorest merely bring people together and in a variety of ways (lectures, films, tapes, handout materials), tell people what they ought to be doing, and then hope that people will go back home and do what they have been told.

The best of the programs do the following: (1) they allow people to talk about and explore the reasons for their current performance; (2) they allow people to set their own goals for improved performance; (3) they allow people to begin to try out and practice new ways of behaving as they have some experience with new behaviors; and (4) they provide feedback on the effectiveness of new behaviors.

All of these programs, both good and bad, have the problem of learning transfer. Whenever we take people off the job and try to train them for that job in a program setting, we face the problem that they may behave very well in the safe program; but, when they return to the real situation, the press

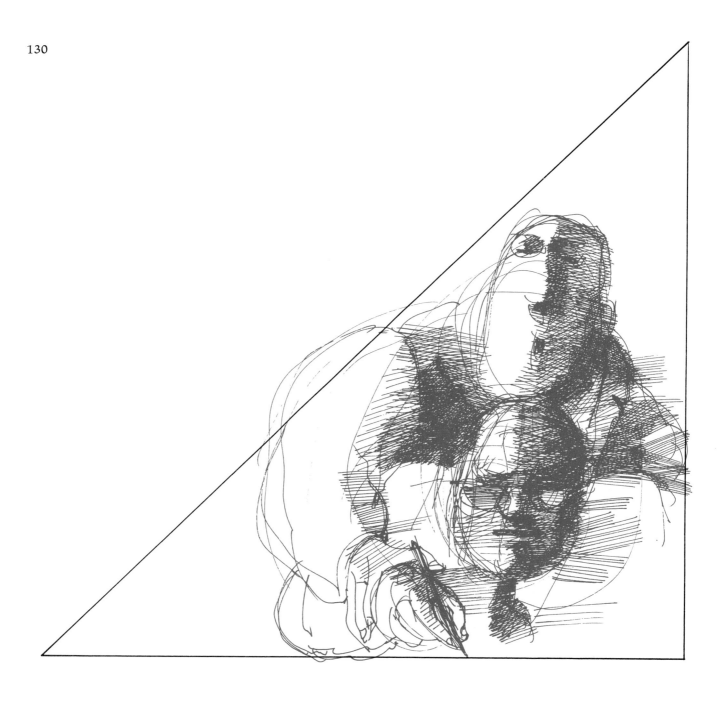

of many forces causes them to revert back to old ways of behaving. A good deal of research has indicated that people need to have some support and encouragement in the ongoing situation in order to successfully try out and continue new behaviors.

Coaching

Coaching is an old principle of training and derives from the notion of the athletic coach who practices his players during the week, watches the performance during the game — takes people out of the game and gives them instructions and then puts them back in the game. Following the game, they have a critique of performance, more practice, another game, whatever.

While this is an old principle, it is losing ground. Many situations are such that it is not easy to have a "coach" present watching the performance, and giving new instructions. However, many organizations are trying types of coaching; some are assigning new men to experienced older men for a period of training with this "coach."

Consultants

A type of coach is the consultant who comes from outside the existing organization, watches the ongoing performance, and then gives instruction, guidance, directions, and practice sessions, in an attempt to help improve the performance level.

Job Rotation

Somewhat akin to coaching is job rotation where a person who must supervise a wide variety of people and positions spends some time in each job; so he has some firsthand experience in this job, hopefully under the coaching of a good person.

What Is Involved in a Good Training Program?

Having examined a number of aspects of training and training programs, we need to spell out what constitutes a good training program.

Examination of Performance

A good training program will include an opportunity for the person being trained to examine his current performance level in such a way that he clearly sees what he is doing that is effective and what he is doing that needs improving. An important aspect of this process is feedback— the receiving of data from others as to how one is doing in his job. In order to examine one's performance there needs to be a process of data collection; feedback is one aspect of it. One of the weaknesses of many training programs is that people undergoing the training are not really sure what areas they need to improve; there has been little or no collection of data or feedback about one's performance.

Establishment of Change Goals

If a person is to improve his performance, he needs to know not only what he is currently doing, but he needs also to decide himself what his goals for improvement are. This means that he must know his own potentials and limitations so that he can set realistic goals for himself. This is an important part of motivation — for a person to supply his own motivation out of his own set of commitments. Motivation and commitment are less if someone else establishes the change goals and tries to get people to change even though they have no real involvement in the change process.

Motivation and commitment are less if someone else establishes the change goals.

New Information, Ideas, Principles, Directions

Once a person sees what he has been doing that needs improving and has set some goals for his own improvement, he can now use some new ideas, new directions, and new principles. Until the first two conditions have been met, it is hard for a person to know if he really needs new information or just how he can use it. Too many programs consist of funneling new information to people before they have any real feel for how they can use it effectively in their programs, or if they need it.

People do not change easily or all at once. Most of us need to have a chance to try out new ways, to get familiar with new procedures, to go through them several times to become familiar and comfortable with new ways of doing things. Too often the training program does not build in this part. The problem of training meetings or workshops away from the actual work situation is that there is no chance to really try out new ways of behaving in the work situation. We are just hoping that people have enough courage and insight to go back home and try out a new behavior when it has never been used before in that setting.

This is one of the hardest conditions to establish — allowing people the right to try out new things, to make mistakes, and to learn from them.

Climate

If a person is going to feel free to try out new things and to experiment with new behaviors, and if others are going to give him feedback about how he is doing, then there must be the right kind of climate in the situation. People must feel free enough to try new things. If the climate is threatening and one feels he is being criticized or evaluated negatively, or that people are going to laugh at or mock him if he makes a mistake, then that person will probably feel very reluctant to change his behavior.

The above conditions seem to be best applied right in the work setting. If conditions can be created in the ongoing work situation where the right kind of climate can be created and people can honestly look at their own performance and then someone — a coach, consultant, etc. — can give them new ideas or directions and if the conditions continue to be safe, it may be possible for the person to try out new ways of behaving that have a chance to continue.

Follow Up

Once a program of improvement is started, it needs to be continued. A follow up on the change

People must feel free enough to try new things.

process is important. The follow-up program essentially means a repeat of the training conditions. Periodically the person in training needs to examine his performance, get more feedback and data, get new information, and then try again and again. If this process can get started and can be built into the work activities of each person, then it is possible to create a situation where every person is constantly working on his own improvement.

Organization Support

Too often training programs fail because the person returning to his job after a training program is not supported in the new activities suggested by the training. New behavior, programs, and actions need to be encouraged and supported by one's superiors, peers, and subordinates. Team training (the training of a total work unit) is one way to help ensure that training is utilized in the organization. If one's superior supports the program of training, he can lend organization support by rewarding the new behaviors through the regular organization channels.

Training programs fail because the person returning to his job after a training program is not supported.

The Helping Relationship

According to most people, effectively working with other people requires that we first "build a good relationship." Other ways of stating this same axiom are "develop rapport," or "establish a good climate," or "gain their confidence." Unfortunately most discussions stop at this point as though the subject were covered having stated the principle. Each person is left to his own devices as to what should be done in establishing what is the critical base of the whole subsequent working relationship.

What is important in building this effective or "good" relationship? Fortunately there is some good research and theory to help develop an answer to this question.

Individual Needs

As the person who desires to be helpful contacts another person, he should keep in mind that this other person represents a collection of needs or conditions of the organism that demands some satisfaction; or, if satisfaction is not practical, then some adjustment must be made. These needs have been described in many ways and there is no final definitive cataloging of the need system. One useful model is that developed by Maslow (1953:370-396) who felt that there is a hierarchy of human needs, each need in the hierarchy dependent on those below it in the system. The base of the need system is formed by certain physiological needs — needs for nourishment, rest, air, elimination, and so on. When these needs are met, another set predominates the concern of the person, namely safety needs which are needs to be protected against danger, threats, or deprivations of various kinds.

When one is secure and physiologically satisfied, the third set of needs come into play, social needs, which are demands to belong, to be liked, to be included with others. Above the social needs are needs centered around one's feelings of self, called ego needs, which involve needs to have self-respect and self-confidence, to feel that one is worthwhile, and also needs for recognition, status, and the respect of others.

Finally, according to Maslow, at the pinnacle of the need system are needs of self-fulfillment, needs for achieving one's full potential, and satisfying one's longings for achieving what is best within him.

While this conception of the human needs system may not be entirely accurate or adequate, still it points out one of the important factors in the building of the relationship with others. If it is true that each person has a collection of personal needs, then it would seem that the person who would not meet or even violate these needs would not build the same type of relationship as one who could meet the needs of another person. Too often in the interest of getting the job done, the concentration is on the task, and not in taking into account the needs of the person. In building a helping relationship, it is especially important to take into account the social, ego, and self-actualizing needs of the other.

Individual Values

Each person is not only a complex system of needs, he is also a system of values. Every person has a set of feelings about certain ideas, concepts, situations, or activities that represents points of concern, of worth, and of importance. Individual value systems vary, and what is valuable to one person may not be valuable to another. For example, Mr. Andrews may value his privacy, his right to make his own decisions; he may value the opinion of a newspaper columnist, and the efficacy of prayer as a means of final answers to questions. Should a person come to be "helpful" with him and not know or try to understand his value system, the helpful person may engage in activities, make remarks, or suggest actions that are in direct opposition to what Mr. Andrews holds to be of value. Should this occur, the prediction would be that the relationship would not be one of rapport or confidence, rather it would be strained, antagonistic, uncooperative, and perhaps even hostile. As in the case

with human needs, the person desiring to build a
good relationship would find it advantageous to
understand the person's value system and to respect
it in the course of the interaction.

Individual Expectations

The individual need system and value system are
independent of the person desiring to build a relationship. They are rather constant factors that are continually in operation. However, another complex of
attitudes is important in the building of an effective
helping relationship, namely the expectations the
client has of the helping person.

Expectations refer to the feeling one person has
that another person should behave in certain ways.
Sometimes expectations are shared — each person
knows what others expect of him and the whole
result is one of cohesion and harmony as people meet
each other's expectations and consequently reward
each other. When expectations are not met, it is
predicted that negative reactions, conflict, and dis-
harmony will result. From this it would appear that
if the change agent (CA) does not meet the expectations of the client or the system members, negative
reactions would occur and the basic relationship would
not be one of rapport, cohesion, or confidence.

It sometimes happens that one person will consciously and deliberately violate or fail to meet the
expectations of another person, but this is the unusual
occurrence. More likely is the probability that when
one person fails to meet the expectations of another
person it results from a lack of information about the
other's expectation system. To ensure a situation of
nonviolation of expectations, the CA must know the
expectations of the system member, as well as the
needs and values of the persons in the system.

Understanding and Meeting Needs, Values, and Expectations

If the above conceptions are valid and people do
indeed have needs, values, and expectations that are

important to them, it would follow that if another person behaves in ways that do not meet needs and violate one's values and expectations that the relationship which would result would not be conducive to effectively working together.

Basic to successful functioning within the boundaries of the needs, values, and expectations systems is understanding what these are in another person. How does one go about finding out these important dimensions from another person?

Some guidelines for gaining this understanding follow:

Leveling. In opening the interaction with the client system, the CA may attempt to start the relationship on the basis that each participant will "level" with the other person. The attempt is to establish a basic ground rule that is fundamental to the whole relationship, namely complete frankness and honesty with each other.

If the client system indicates a willingness to adopt such a ground rule, then the CA may wish to ask the members of the system to let him know honestly how they feel concerning their needs, values, and expectations. He might ask for information such as:

1. When is it most convenient for me to come and work with you? (What are your expectations about time arrangements?)

2. What do you think I ought to do when I work with you?

3. Do you have any apprehensions or feelings of anxiety about having me come?

4. How do you feel about the conditions you have in your system?

5. What bothers you most about your situation in this system?

Sharing. An important part of the leveling process is the reciprocal sharing of data from the CA to the individual. A good working relationship is based on mutual understanding and shared confidence. It is as important for the CA to level with the person as is the reverse. The CA is at something of a disadvantage in sharing ideas, information, and feelings with the person, for his professional role sometimes limits the amount of data he can share. However, the CA may talk with the system members about such things as:

1. What I see my role to be in working with you.
2. What I think a good CA-client relationship should be.
3. Some of the anxieties I have in performing my work.
4. What I see as some of my competencies in working with you.

The keynote here is that both the CA and the individual *begin* their experience by talking about the relationship. The ultimate concern is the achievement of system objectives, but the relationship must be built in order to work effectively on the problems.

Individual Differences

It is a common cliché that "all people are different," but it is important to keep this fact in mind. The individual mix of needs, values, and expectations is going to be different for every person. No one approach will handle every situation. The CA needs to develop or increase his level of sensitivity. *Sensitivity* has been defined as the ability to discriminate clearly among individuals on the basis of their characteristics. Some persons are capable of seeing individual differences more accurately than others and are then able to respond appropriately in light of their understanding. Dubin summarizes this way, "The more successful supervisor may be the one best able to perceive these individual characteristics in order to tailor his own actions to the individual's unique qualities" (1965:39).

If the ability to differentiate between individuals and then to respond appropriately to these differences is an important aspect of the CA-client relationship, then it would seem that increasing this ability would be an important part of the training of persons who must work closely with others. If it is possible to teach people to be more perceptive and sensitive to others, then this training should be part of the program of education for CAs. Persons who are rather rigid and inflexible in their responses to others may have difficulty in making the appropriate modifications for individual differences. Perhaps this inflexibility, if it cannot be modified, should be an important consideration in the selection of CAs whose jobs put them into contact with many different people. Certainly there is some research evidence that sensitivity and flexibility are important in good interpersonal relations, and the question now is *How* to increase these behaviors in the CA.

The Communication of Acceptance

From the fields of counseling and therapy comes the notion of interpersonal acceptance. This involves the subtle communication from one person to another which shows a genuine interest and concern for the person, and more importantly, a willingness to try to understand without evaluation and judgment the other person exactly the way he is.

Behavioral Inputs

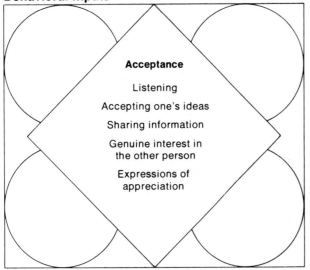

Acceptance

Listening

Accepting one's ideas

Sharing information

Genuine interest in
the other person

Expressions of
appreciation

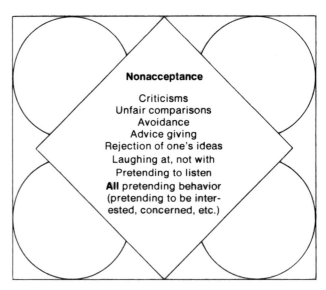

Nonacceptance

Criticisms
Unfair comparisons
Avoidance
Advice giving
Rejection of one's ideas
Laughing at, not with
Pretending to listen
All pretending behavior
(pretending to be interested, concerned, etc.)

Feelings of nonacceptance can be communicated in many ways, both verbally and nonverbally. A common experience of persons working in homes of a different social-class level than their own is a sense of revulsion toward conditions so dissimilar. If a person working with a lower-class family were to react negatively to the unsanitary surroundings in the sense that it would imply "You're dirty and I'm not. I'm better than you are" then one would predict that a feeling of nonacceptance would be established.

What are the behaviors that tend to make a person feel accepted or nonaccepted? The diagram on page 140 may help to look at the behavioral inputs that result in feelings of acceptance or nonacceptance.

Nonacceptance and Acceptance

What are the results of the nonaccepting relationship? It would be predicted that if the system member did not honestly feel acceptance from the CA that some of the following things might occur:

1. *Results of nonacceptance*
   a. Antagonistic feelings
   b. Noncooperation
   c. Avoidance of the person
   d. Little sharing of information
   e. Noncompliance with suggestions or advice
   f. Feelings of relief when the relationship is terminated

All of the above are conditions that would plague the CA and prevent him from accomplishing his goals with the system. On the other hand, if the CA were able to develop the kind of accepting relationship discussed here, we would predict more of the following:

2. *Results of acceptance*
   a. Sharing of information
   b. Cooperation
   c. Feelings of closeness
   d. Willingness to work interdependently
   e. Welcome and anticipation of one's return

As indicated above, the behavioral inputs from the CA to the system influence the feelings of acceptance or nonacceptance. One of the real problems is for the CA to get a clear picture of how his behavior is being experienced by the system members he is trying to help. If the CA thinks his behavioral inputs are appropriate, he will continue to behave this way until he discovers they are not. Some ways of checking one's behavioral inputs include

1. An evaluation questionnaire could be circulated to the system members.

2. Supervisors or an outside person could make a periodic interview to check on the reactions of the system members.

3. It may be possible to have an observer visit the system and watch the CA in action. Following this, an honest exchange of information would be given.

4. It is possible in some cases to tape-record a visit and have a group of colleagues critique the session. The important thing here is to get an honest evaluation of performance as the work with others progresses.

It is also apparent that building an effective relationship involves not only information about what is needed but also skills in working with others and attitudes appropriate to desiring such a condition. In this respect, training persons to build effective relationships with others requires a concentration on information, skills, and attitudes. Too much of our current learning emphasis is based primarily on the acquiring of information.

References

Dubin, Robert
  1965   Leadership and Productivity. San Francisco: Chandler Publishing Company: 39.

Maslow, Abraham H.
  1943   "A theory of human motivation." Psychological Review 50:370-396.

Much has been written about the role of the change agent particularly from a theoretical point of view; however, the ongoing specifics of the change agent as he works in an organization have not been clearly set forth. This is an attempt to show the step-by-step actions of a consultant as he works with an organization to bring about improvement. This is my own experience.

Phase 1. The Initial Contact

In this particular situation, I was contacted by two members of a government agency who held positions in the training, personnel, and public relations areas. The director of training and the director of public relations came to me and told me they were interested in establishing a development program for top management in their agency. They asked if I would be interested in such a program.

Question 1. The first question that I must ask and answer for myself and the client is: Am I capable of providing the kind of resource this particular client needs?

With this question in mind I told these two directors that I would be interested in working with such a training program only if the training the agency management needed was the type I was equipped to supply. This was agreeable to them, but they asked the next question.

Question 2. How can we determine just what training or development experience the management or client needs?

This is not an easy question, for there are at least these possibilities:

1. There may be some objective needs of that agency that could be determined by an outside, impartial analysis of the total functioning of the agency.

2. There may be needs of the management personnel that they feel are subjective to them but may

not be the needs that are "objectively needed."

3. It is also possible that the subjective and objective needs are fairly close together.

In terms of dealing with this question I made the following arrangement with the two who contacted me: I would enter into a data-gathering process by interviewing all the top management who would normally be involved in a development program. I would try to be as objective as possible in gathering the information. I would tabulate and analyze the data to see what these men felt were their needs and the needs of the agency for development. I would present the data to them, and on the basis of this information determine if the kind of resource I would supply would be compatible with the needs so uncovered.

I indicated immediately to them that if the problems of the agency were in such areas as fiscal, budgeting, state-federal relations, aspects of technical planning, and programming peculiar to the work of that agency then I would not be a good resource. Using the Mann (1965) model — that the person in management needs a combination of technical, interpersonal, and cognitive skills — I indicated that if their management felt they needed technical training or they needed to have a perspective about the total functioning of their agency and its programs, I would not be a good resource. If, however, their needs were in the area of interpersonal behavior — a lack of competence in dealing with human problems — then I felt I could be of assistance to them.

Phase 2. Data Collection

The consultant could bias the data.

From a strictly objective, scientific point of view, the collection of data should have been conducted by someone who would not be involved in the programs. It is possible that I, the consultant, could bias the data in directions I desired, particularly when there is a possibility of gain for me. While this was desirable, it was not done. Trained personnel for collecting such data were not readily available. The work needed to be done immediately in light of time and budget requirements.

I made the decision to collect the data myself because I felt I could competently interview and analyze the data. I felt I could be objective within a suitable level. I did not personally "need" the contract from a financial point of view because my livelihood was not dependent on having or not having this contract.

Question 3. How can I become acquainted with the management personnel in such a way as to build a level of trust and confidence and obtain the information necessary to plan an effective future program?

I knew that my initial contact with the persons would be critical in terms of establishing a basis for an ongoing relationship. I, therefore, resolved to completely level with each person and to explain exactly my position and what I was trying to do.

Appointments were set up for me by the training officer, and I began the interviews. With each manager I explained: I was not hired to do a total development program. I was only trying to find out what they felt were their needs and those of the agency. In this way I would be able to make an assessment of the kind of program, if any, that was needed for improving their functioning and that of the agency.

Interview Questions

I used the following questions as a general guide in each interview:

a. *What is your job in the agency? Would you describe it to me?*
b. *What do you think are the biggest problems you face in doing your job?*
c. *What do you think you need personally in the way of training to improve your functioning in your job?*
d. *What do you think are the biggest problems facing the agency?*
e. *What do you think would help the agency to function better?*

These were the general questions. I felt free to question further within the areas developed by the initial questions. Each interview lasted about two hours.

In addition to the interview data I also spent considerable time with the training director getting a picture of the agency organization, its programs, policies, and procedures. I also had available to me an employee attitude survey taken some eight years earlier. Besides this information, I read the agency handbook and other literature describing its work.

From the interviews I tabulated the data by problems or needs mentioned in the interviews. I listed all items of concern mentioned by three or more people and put them on newsprint.

Phase 3. Decision

A meeting was then called of all top-level managers. At this meeting I presented the list of problems or concerns. I pointed out those problems in the agency that I felt I could help and those that were not in my area of competency. I listed for them all of the general areas of their concerns that I felt were within my resource capacity to help, such as

1. Dealing with conflict
2. Improving communications and feedback
3. Improving staff meetings and the procedures for planning
4. Improving the decision-making process
5. Widening the base of acceptance in the management staff
6. Improving motivation

During the meeting I was concerned with the next question:

Question 4. If I work with this staff, how can I develop a relationship where they are committed to investing themselves in a program of training?

I felt that if this group were to have a program of training and if they were to develop any commitment to the program, they would have to decide if they wanted me to work with them. I told them, following the data presentation, they should decide whether they wanted to follow a training program in the areas of my competence. Further, I indicated that I did not want the agency director, the training director, or others to put pressures on them to go ahead with this. It should be the consent of each person to participate or not in such a program, if it were accepted. Following these remarks I left the room telling them that I would like them to make a decision and inform me at my home later. I tried to assure them that they should do what they felt was best for the agency — not make a decision to please me or anyone else. With that I left and returned home. The next day I was contacted by the training officer who reported that after an hour's discussion the program was unanimously accepted and that all could participate.

I left the room.

Phase 4. The Development Program

At the decision-making meeting I had outlined a proposed development program within my areas of competence so the group would have some basis for making a decision about participating in the program. I felt it was not fair to ask them to decide for or against a program without some indication as to what the program would be like. The proposed program was as follows:

Proposed Management and Organization Development Program

I. Initial Three-Day Laboratory
   A. The purpose of this intensive period was to provide an opportunity for participants and the consultant to create a situation where all could examine and begin to work on the following:
      1. The level of acceptance in management.
      2. Level of communication in the staff.
      3. Decision-making procedures in the staff.
      4. Areas of conflict among staff members.
      5. The interpersonal competence level and management style of each staff member.

B. At the laboratory certain new concepts of organization and management would be introduced.

II. Follow-up Consultation

Following the laboratory, the consultant would meet with each participant to review with him the findings of the laboratory period, to help him plan a program for his own improvement and the improvement of his department.

III. Short Seminars

In addition to the follow-up consultations, some seminar periods would be held to talk about problems of organization and management.

Question 5. What kind of training program can be developed to involve the staff members at a significant level so learning can begin?

In discussions with the agency administrator and the training director, it was suggested that T-Group or sensitivity group training was somewhat suspect

Laboratory Design FIRST DAY

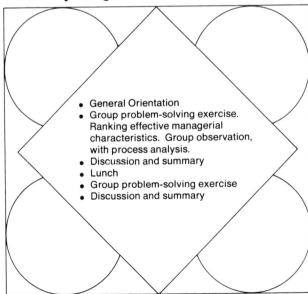

- General Orientation
- Group problem-solving exercise. Ranking effective managerial characteristics. Group observation, with process analysis.
- Discussion and summary
- Lunch
- Group problem-solving exercise
- Discussion and summary

among some of the management staff, and it was recommended that this format not be used. They were referring particularly to the completely unstructured T-Group situation which was not thought to help focus on the problems of the organization. I agreed not to have the completely unstructured situation and to center the three-day program on matters of concern to the staff members.

The above design allowed me to examine with the group most of the problem areas that fell within my realm of concern. The first day was a relatively structured day — and nonthreatening; it allowed me to further build a relationship with the staff and to watch them work together on some imposed problems. The laboratory allowed us to examine the nature of problem solving, planning, decision making, conflict areas within the staff, level of acceptance of staff members, and to open channels of communication and feedback to various staff members.

Laboratory Design

SECOND DAY

- Lecture: Management style
- Group Discussion: Each manager describes his own management style, how he felt he functioned, and his assessments of his own strengths and weaknesses.
- Lunch
- Continuation of group discussion

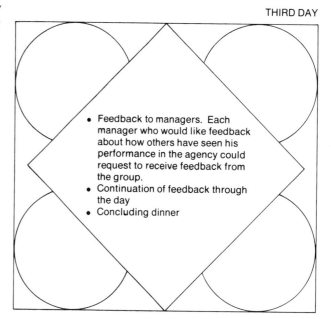

THIRD DAY

- Feedback to managers. Each manager who would like feedback about how others have seen his performance in the agency could request to receive feedback from the group.
- Continuation of feedback through the day
- Concluding dinner

Phase 5. The Follow-up Program

Question 6. What type of follow-up activity will help implement the gains of the laboratory in the back-home situation?

By its very nature, a laboratory program conducted in house with people who have ongoing relationships has certain advantages. Any improvements in relationships gained in the program have great possibilities for continuing. However, I felt that each manager needed to have an opportunity to review the feedback given him during the laboratory and to have help in planning a program of improvement based on this new information.

During the discussion of management style and the feedback sessions that followed, I took extensive notes on each person. I had a complete description of his self-perception and also the feedback of the staff about him. Within a month after the laboratory, I began another series of consultation interviews with each participant.

In these sessions I reviewed with each manager what he had said about himself and then what others had shared with him in the way of feedback about his performance. This information was discussed at length and I asked each man, "In light of this information, what do you think you should be doing to improve your performance?" I then tried to help each person think through a concrete plan for improvement based on the feedback given.

Of critical importance were the sessions spent with the top men in the agency, the administrator and assistant administrator. Both of these men accepted the development program and openly supported all activities. A great deal of feedback was given in the sessions to both of them, and both developed concrete plans to improve. Support from the top levels seemed to encourage others to give and receive feedback more openly and to plan for change with some optimism that change could be effected.

"What do you think you should be doing to improve your performance?"

Question 7. How can I leave the client functioning effectively after my role as consultant has ended?

In the consulting program it is important that the relationship with the client system be terminated at a point where the client system has developed such a level of autonomy of action that it can continue a program of improvement without being dependent on the presence of the consultant.

Termination was not considered until each manager had a concrete plan for his own improvement, an intermediate progress report had been circulated from the consultant to the total staff on what had been happening in the development program thus far, and then a final written report given to all, outlining the program, the gains made, and the work still to be done as seen by the consultant.

A formal termination session was then held. The final report was reviewed and discussed, followed by a closing dinner.

Discussion — Apparent Gains of the Program

Missing in this training program is an evaluation of the program. This needs to be done, preferably by someone not connected with the training, and at some time period following the training program. Unfortunately, too few organizations have budget and program policies that build in evaluation of programs. Thus any evaluation of the program at this point can only be very subjective at best.

On the basis of my follow-up interviews with each manager, certain gains were commonly mentioned to me as being apparent to them:

1. The administrator had gained a new insight into methods of decision making. He was making a real attempt in staff meetings to arrive at consensus for decisions that effected the total agency or consensus among those who would be affected by the decision.

2. Persons with differences explored in the feed-

back sessions had gone to each other and continued to work on ways of resolving differences.

3. Some persons had made some direct behavior changes, e.g., getting out of the office more and visiting others, consulting with others before making decisions, speaking up more in staff meetings, taking more time to listen to subordinates.

4. Some persons had been able to clarify certain of their staff functions in the agency as a result of being able to talk about their roles.

5. Certain of the younger and newer members of the management staff felt greater acceptance and more ease in the staff group than before and as a result felt freer to contribute in the staff meetings.

Reference

Mann, Floyd C.
　　1965　　"Toward an understanding of the leadership role in formal organization." in R. Dubin, Leadership and Productivity. San Francisco: Chandler Publishing Co.: 68-103.

Central to the whole area of human relations training with the emphasis on the training group (and to an important degree in discussion groups, group-centered classroom situations and group counseling or therapy) is the role of trainer. While some training programs have eliminated the trainer, in most other group-centered training programs he still represents an important element in the total learning environment (Blake and Mouton, 1962: 61-77).

For those involved in conducting training groups, certain key questions concerning the behavior of the trainer have consistently confronted the trainer, or educator as Argyris (1962:153) prefers. Some of the questions have been: 1. How active should I be in participating in the group? 2. What kinds of things should I do when I intervene in the activities of the group? 3. What kind of relationship should I establish with the group members — should I stay aloof or become one of the group?

It is with the second of these questions that this paper is concerned. What are the types of interventions open to a trainer as he conducts his group, and what are the probable implications and consequences of these various types of interventions. It is hoped that this inventory of interventions may allow more systematic analysis of trainer behavior and its resulting effects.

Types of Interventions

Content Focus

Here the trainer actually comments on or contributes to the topic of discussion. If the group is discussing a topic such as "How should an effective supervisor behave," a content intervention by the trainer would be for him to share an experience, some research data, or his opinion concerning the topic at hand.

*Revised. Reprinted by special permission from Human Relations Training News, "An inventory of trainer interventions," William G. Dyer 7 (Spring 1963).

What are the types
of interventions
open to a trainer?

Comment: Since the behavior of the trainer is often seen as a model for group members to follow, a content intervention may give legitimacy to the topic and perpetuate its discussion. Since the focus of most group-training groups is on what is happening in the group "here and now," a content intervention may keep the group from looking at its own processes. For the person conducting a discussion group where the focus is on content, the content intervention may contribute to the goals of the group, providing the trainer has not made the contribution another group member might have made.

Process Focus

This type of intervention attempts to shift the focus of the group to what is happening in the group "here and now." One of the most standard of these interventions (almost to the point of becoming a cliché among trainers) is for the trainer to say, "I wonder what is really going on in the group now," or "Why are we doing this?" Others would prefer to focus on process by pointing out a process condition such as, "Were you all aware that only two persons voiced an opinion yet a decision was made?"

Comment: There are a wide variety of ways a trainer may help the group focus on its own processes. The ways actually selected by the trainer are probably determined by his own personal style or in terms of the explicit or implicit strategy he has for bringing about the learnings he desires to develop. Argyris (1962:166-167) has this to say about the process intervention that begins with "I wonder . . ." "I would not [use this phrasing] because this would be dishonest. I am really *not* wondering. I believe I know why they are doing it. And perhaps more important, I believe they feel that I know. Dishonesty does not lead to authentic relationships."

Asking for Feelings

Here the trainer is attempting to draw data out from the group members as to how they feel about

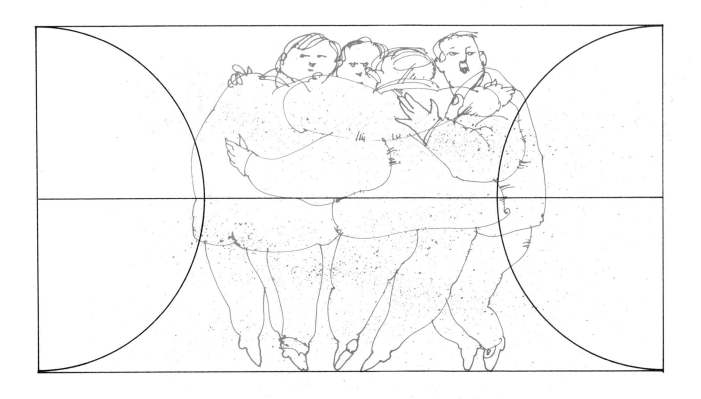

certain conditions or situations that have occurred in the group. An intervention of this type would be, "Ed, how did you feel when the group rejected your idea?" This is really a type of process intervention, for it often leads to a looking at what has happened, but in addition it solicits member reactions to what has happened.

Comment: Some trainers and many persons participating in training groups find the sharing of feelings the most interesting part of the training process. For some, it is the first time they have been able to find out how others feel about how they behave. Certainly this is an important and legitimate learning goal. However, if the trainer concentrates on this type of intervention, he may neglect a number of other important facets of group action. This matter of focus on feeling versus group variables has been an important issue in human relations training (Bradford, Benne, and Gibb, 1964).

Direction Giving

At times the trainer may intervene to give the group certain suggestions, directions, procedures, or ground rules which influence the direction the group takes. Early in the group's life the trainer may structure the group by having the members write out name cards, use a tape recorder, or stop at some given time. At other times, he may suggest they use a group observer, provide observation forms, try out an exercise, or role play.

Comment: Trainers differ in how they use direction-giving interventions. Some offer direction only in form of suggestions while others by virtue of their status position arbitrarily impose certain actions on the group members. Both positions have a rationale — those preferring suggestions feel the group members should be the ones to make their own decisions, while those favoring an imposed direction feel the group members should have the experience of dealing with this type of behavior and learn how to cope with such forced directions if they dislike it.

It would appear that if a trainer has high needs to control he may satisfy these needs by intervening often with direction giving, or he may recognize this need in himself and overreact, not supplying direction to the group when it may be helpful. A critical point in training often comes when the group is floundering and is not learning. The trainer must then decide either to let the group try to work through its own impasse or to supply some direction. This involves the whole problem of perhaps reinforcing dependency, but on the other hand permitting the group to waste time and wallow in frustration beyond that which is desirable for learning. In such situations, the trainer must consider such factors as the length of the training program, his judgment as to the level of dependency, the resources available to the group, and his own tolerance for ambiguity.

Direct Feedback

At certain times the trainer may intervene by giving direct feedback to a group member or to the group as a whole. When and how this is done again depends on the strategy of the trainer.

Comment: Some trainers prefer to give direct feedback early in the life of the group, both as a model to group members and to legitimize this type of response. Others prefer to wait until they have worked through some of the authority problems with group members, fearing the effects of feedback from the trainer until the authority issue has been dealt with. Here again the trainer is faced with a dilemma. Group members are often anxious, and properly so, to know how the trainer, who is really the only trained person in the group, sees the group and the individual members. However, the reactions of the trainer are often no more valid or important than the feedback of other group members. The trainer must somehow share his feedback and, at the same time, get the group to gather and appreciate the feedback data of all group members.

Feedback to the group involves the expression of

The trainer must then decide either to let the group try to work through its own impasse or to supply some direction.

the trainer's reactions to what has been going on in the group. The same issues involved in expressing feedback to individuals are connected with giving group feedback.

Cognitive Orientations

Occasionally, the trainer may feel it important to give some general "theory" or information elaborating or clarifying or providing insight into an experience the group has had. Some may give a "lecturette" while others may talk briefly with the group.

Comment: Again the trainer must face the question — if I take time to provide the insight, will this heighten the learning process, or will the participants learn more if they can glean the same insight from their own experiences? The trainer must be careful that he does not monopolize the group by giving a great deal of cognitive information (perhaps satisfying his own need to be seen as an expert) but really minimizing the benefit that comes from persons learning for themselves.

Performing Group Task-Maintenance Functions

According to Benne and Sheats (1948:42-47), there are a series of various task and maintenance activities that should be performed if a group is going to accomplish its task and maintain itself as an effective human system. Assuming the task of the training group is to facilitiate the learnings of the participants, the trainer often intervenes and performs a number of the task-maintenance functions necessary to promote learning.

Task Functions (These and the list of maintenance functions are taken largely from Benne and Sheats [1948]).

1. *Opinion seeking.* The trainer here may ask other group members for their reactions to what has happened in the group.

2. *Opinion giving.* The trainer here may share his opinion as to what he thinks is going on in the group.

3. *Initiating.* This is similar to part of direction

giving mentioned above. The authors say of this role, "(it) may take the form of suggestions of a new group goal or a new definition of the problem. It may take the form of a suggested solution or some way of handling a difficulty that the group has encountered. Or it may take the form of a proposed new procedure for the group, a new way of organizing the group for the task ahead " (Benne and Sheats, 1948:44).

4. *Elaborating.* An intervention of this kind might be to expand or develop an idea already presented by others.

5. *Coordinating.* Trainer may try to pull together different ideas or suggestions already introduced into the group.

6. *Summarizing.* Here the trainer might attempt to summarize what he feels has been going on in the group, or what he feels have been some of the important insights gained.

7. *Consensus testing.* In this intervention the trainer may ask the group members if they were all in agreement concerning a certain decision or action effected in the group.

8. *Procedural technician.* The person performing this function "expedites group movement by doing things for the group — performing routine tasks, e.g., distributing materials, or manipulating objects for the group, rearranging the seating or running the recording machine, etc." (Benne and Sheats, 1948: 44). This represents something of a physical intervention in the group.

9. *Reality Testing.* When it has been suggested by the group that a member, or the group, behave in a certain way or try out certain actions, the trainer may intervene and help members explore whether this action is really possible or desirable.

Maintenance Functions:

1. *Encouraging.* The trainer would intervene by praising, supporting, or otherwise accepting the contributions of group members.

2. *Harmonizing.* Here the trainer would intervene

by trying to reconcile differences that occur between group members.

3. *Gate keeping.* The trainer intervention would be to encourage or facilitate the participation of group members.

4. *Standard setting.* An intervention of this type would call for the trainer to express a standard or norm that he feels would help the group reach its learning goals (Bradford, Benne, and Gibb, 1964).

Individual Roles

Benne and Sheats (1948:42-47) also mention that sometimes individuals use the group to satisfy individual needs and perform certain actions. They classify such a person as the aggressor, blocker, recognition seeker, self-confessor, playboy, dominator, and so on. Trainers may intervene at times in this manner, but it is questionable whether these types of interventions facilitate the learnings of group members.

Comment: When and how often the trainer performs various task-maintenance functions for the group depends on the strategy of the trainer. Some will intervene extensively early in the life of the training along the task-maintenance dimensions not only to provide a model to the group participants but also because the trainer feels it is important that certain of these functions be performed. Since group members have not yet developed an understanding or an ability to perform these functions, the trainer supplies the needed behaviors, at least as he sees they are needed. As group members develop greater ability to perform these group functions, the trainer may reduce his own efforts in this area. Then, when certain functions are needed, the trainer may intervene by focusing on process and asking why certain functions have not been performed in the group.

Diagnostic Intervention.

From time to time the trainer may come into the group with a diagnosis of what he sees happening in the group. He may do this by suggesting a hypothe-

Sometimes individuals use the group to satisfy individual needs.

sis or series of hypotheses as to what has contributed to the situation or condition under diagnosis. For example, the group members may recognize and be at a loss over a condition of apathy that exists in the group; no one seems to be interested, involved, or active. The trainer may then intervene with a diagnosis of the situation with something like this: "There are a number of possibilities why the group is apathetic. One hypothesis is that our goals are either not clear or are too broad. Another hypothesis is that we are afraid that if we start to work again old conflicts may be reopened." Following this, the trainer may ask for other possibilities from group members or suggest that they examine their own reactions as to what are the forces connected with the apathetic condition. The intervention is a part of his strategy to get the group to enter into a process of diagnosing group problems.

Comment: The diagnostic intervention is somewhere between opinion giving and developing a level of theory or insight (cognitive orientation). The diagnostic intervention is more an exploratory, suggesting, hypothesizing type of comment. The purpose is to suggest ways of looking at and trying to understand what has been happening in the group.

Protection Intervention

This type of intervention has been suggested by Blake (Bradford, Benne, and Gibb, 1964) who feels the trainer should intervene at certain points to protect certain individual members. This type of intervention may or may not be in the repertoire of the trainer, depending on his theory of training. The intervention may call for the trainer to keep members from "overexposing" their behavior, that is, sharing personal incidents, feelings, reactions, that may not facilitate learnings appropriate to the goals of the training group. Overexposure of behavior may create a group situation with which neither the members nor the trainer is capable of dealing.

A trainer may also feel a need to protect a group

member if he feels that feedback to the person is ill timed or unnecessarily severe. Or the trainer may deem it necessary to protect the individuality of a member, to allow him to maintain his own individual identity despite certain group pressures to conform.

Comment: Some trainers would not use this intervention, but would, when a situation arose calling for protection, focus on the process amd ask the group if the type of behavior they were engaging in was really appropriate to the goals. A direct protection intervention would call for the trainer to say, "Joe, I think you are going too far at this point." This may really represent only a special type of feedback intervention to the group or to a group member.

Interventions and Strategy

The trainer intervention is only part of the total strategy of the trainer. *Strategy* is the overall plan the trainer has as to how he proposes to bring about the learning goals he has established. It involves such factors as: 1. timing — when and how often does the trainer intervene? 2. issues — around what concerns does he intervene? 3. emotion — how much of the trainer's own emotional makeup and reactions are funneled into the group (his use of humor, anger, praise, warmth)? 4. structure — how much control and direction does the trainer maintain over the group? 5. interpersonal relations — what is the nature of the relationship with group members? Does one try to become a group member, maintain his trainer status uniquely, participate with group members outside the group? 6. theory of individual and group behavior — the trainer's own orientation concerning individual and group dynamics will determine in part what the trainer "sees" going on, around what concerns he will try to focus, and what learnings he will emphasize.

One of the difficult questions in training is, "What strategy or strategies are the most effective in bringing about the desired learnings?" Thus far, little attempt has been made to answer this question objec-

tively. At this point, at least, training is much more
an art than a science. While it may never be possible
or desirable to reduce training to a standardized set
of responses, still, if more trainers are to be developed
and training improved, there must be some attempts
to ascertain what type of trainer style or strategy
produces the maximum learning.

One way to objectify training for research and
analysis purposes is to systematically observe and
catalog the trainer's intervention along the dimensions mentioned above to see what pattern of intervention maximizes certain measured learning goals.

Interventions and the Trainer

In an interesting study, Reisel (1962:93-108) has
pointed out some important effects that the trainer's
personality has on the types of interventions the
trainer makes. Reisel shows that in addition to the
strategy the trainer holds, either explicitly or implicitly, there are certain forces within the trainer himself
that influence his training behavior. The trainer will
intervene in terms of his own needs to control, to be
accepted and liked, and to succeed. He has his own
peculiar patterns of responding to anxiety, conflict,
and ambiguity. The trainer may not be at all aware
as to how these internal forces influence his behavior
in the training process.

In addition to these more deep-seated dimensions,
the trainer also has certain language and speech
patterns, certain physical mannerisms, and certain
gesture patterns that also become part of the intervention. Thus the type of intervention — how it is
used in the strategy of the trainer — plus certain
personality effects of the trainer himself combine to
influence the effect of the intervention on the group
at the time.

By the use of an intervention inventory it may be
possible to bring to light some of the personality
factors influencing the training. One would hypo-
thesize that the trainer with high needs to control
might use more direction giving, cognitive orienta-

tion, direct feedback, and summarizing interventions. The trainer who avoids conflicts and feelings may find it more comfortable to make content and direction interventions and to perform harmonizing functions when conflict occurs.

Summary

An important part of the current training process is the influence of the trainer on the training group. Since the trainer's primary effect is through the interventions he makes in the course of the group's activities, it may be valuable to more systematically study the nature of these interventions, how they are used, and their subsequent effect. This is an attempt to catalog these interventions with some suggestions as to how this inventory might be utilized in further research on the role of the trainer.

References

Argyris, Chris
   1962   Interpersonal Competence and Organizational Effectiveness. Homewood, Illinois: Irwin-Dorsey Press: 153, 166-167.

Benne, Kenneth D., and P. Sheats
   1948   "Functional roles of group members." The Journal of Social Issues 4(Spring):42-47.

Blake, Robert R., and Jane S. Mouton
   1962   "The instrumented training laboratory." in Issues in Training. Washington: National Training Laboratories: 61-77.

Bradford, Leland P., Kenneth D. Benne, and Jack R. Gibb (eds.)
   1964   T-Group Theory and Laboratory Method. New York. Wiley and Sons

Reisel, J.
   1962   "Observations on the trainer role: a case study." Leadership and Organization: A Behavioral Science Approach. McGraw-Hill. Reprinted in Issues in Training: 93-108.

Today many people are engaging in activities designed to help improve that basic fundamental human institution — the family. Some "experts" have claimed that the modern family is losing its importance in the lives of people, since schools, churches, clubs, organizations, police, government, and so forth, are taking over many of the functions of the earlier family system. Others maintain that in fact the family is more important now than ever before. We live in a period of increasing urbanization — the mass society of the "lonely crowd." People do not know their neighbors as before, and today's urban youngster can be in foreign territory only three blocks away from his home or apartment. There are too few people around who are truly concerned about the child — aunts, uncles, grandparents do not live in nearby homes. We sing nostalgically about the old days when at holidays we would go "over the river and through the woods to grandmother's house." With this loss of immediate supportive family and neighbors, the burden of love, affection, discipline, character development, meeting of needs, and solving of problems has fallen on the family members remaining — father, mother, and children. This basic unit often needs help in order to meet the complex and critical issues that confront it. Differing professionals and interested parties are trying to help in homes and families. People such as ministers, doctors, social workers, nurses, and organization members, such as the PTA or church memberships are all attempting to work with families in a way that will help that most important unit become a more viable and effective base for dealing with the problems and concerns that confront it.

Helping Families

How does one person help another? Too often the person who comes into a family situation is seen as the expert, and the reaction to the expert can be either one of hostility and suspicion, or one of overwhelming acceptance with an accompanying depen-

**Dependency
can be flattering.**

dency on the expert to handle all of the problems.

How does the Change Agent (CA) deal with the matter of dependency on him? Here the CA must have some insights about himself. One of the ways of handling dependency is to encourage it. This strategy would be characteristic of a person who finds great satisfaction in having persons dependent on him. Dependency can be flattering. Some research has indicated that people can in many ways encourage others to be dependent while at the same time deny it.

Another possible strategy for dealing with dependency is to reject the dependent person — hold him at arm's length, refuse to enter into any type of close relationship that would foster or support any dependency at all. This process may eliminate dependency but may also lead to two equally uncomfortable consequences: (1) a situation of counter dependency may occur where the person with the problem is rebellious, negative, and resistant to anything the CA has to offer, or (2) a sense of apathy, isolation, or noninvolvement between the person and CA, where the person remains aloof, feeling that the CA does not really want to understand him or accept him and does not really want to help him.

The problem is this: How can the CA build an accepting, supportive, helping relationship with the person without building such a dependency relationship that he cannot finally leave the family functioning independently?

Parsons and Fox (1958) suggest two behaviors that are important in this connection. One, the helping person will adhere scrupulously to a professional attitude, that is, respond consistently as an interested, concerned professional and not be trapped into behaving in ways that are not consistent with professional conduct. Two, the person who is helping the one with the problem introduces conditional rewards, particularly approving the person for gaining insight into his own situation and behavior. These responses are consistent with general practices according to some therapeutic models.

Trust Model

STEP
1

BASIC CONDITIONS

Acceptance or Trust

DESIRED CONSEQUENCES	**DEVIANT CONSEQUENCES**
Acceptance and trust of others, understanding, empathy	Distrust of others, fear, resistance, suspicion

STEP
2

BASIC CONDITIONS

Data Flow

DESIRED CONSEQUENCES	**DEVIANT CONSEQUENCES**
Open, two-way communications, with wide sharing of important, sensitive information	Closed, restricted, one-way communications, little sharing of real feelings or sensitive information

STEP
3

BASIC CONDITIONS

Goal Setting and Decision Making

DESIRED CONSEQUENCES	**DEVIANT CONSEQUENCES**
Person sets own goals, participates in making decisions	Goals set by others, decisions made by others

STEP
4

BASIC CONDITIONS

Control

DESIRED CONSEQUENCES	**DEVIANT CONSEQUENCES**
Self-control, interdependence	Imposed control, checking up on, following around, threatening

Gibb's Trust Model

Jack R. Gibb (Bradford, Benne, and Gibb, 1964:679–710) has suggested another model for looking at the sequential steps that lead finally to a situation where a person functions in a mature way, being neither dependent nor counter dependent, but appropriately interdependent. That is, he is capable of accepting help when it is appropriate and moving ahead on his own when that is called for.

The final condition of mature self-control is based on successfully achieving the conditions specified at the prior three levels. The basic underpinning of the whole developmental sequence is a condition of basic understanding and trust; hence the term *Trust Model* has been applied to Gibb's formulation.

Each condition is dependent on the prior condition; so this suggests the sequence of problems that face the person in a helping role as to what are the problems, actions, and behaviors with which he must deal in working with others. Our concern here is to apply this model to the area of the CA-family relationship and see what implications this model has for the training and functioning of CAs, particularly those who must deal with the family in the home setting. As has been earlier pointed out, the home setting is probably the most difficult setting for achieving the end result of self-control. Let us take each condition in sequence and look at its implications for the helping person.

Acceptance and Trust

"Can I trust him?"

According to this model, the initial basic concern that people have as they encounter each other, and in the case in point, when the person first faces the CA, is, "Who is this person, what does he want, what is he going to try to do to me?" And along with such questions as, "Can I trust him? Will he tell me the truth? Should I tell him everything?" and further, "Will he really help me? Will he understand how I feel?" Somehow the CA must anticipate these concerns and deal with them successfully. Gibb (Bradford, Benne, and Gibb, 1964:300-302), in his research, found that in the area of trust that the law of reciprocity seems to operate. That is, people tend to respond in kind, and, when they are treated with acceptance and are trusted, they tend to accept and trust in return.

Almost all new CAs facing their first experience in this field are counseled by their instructors to learn to *accept the people they visit in the conditions they find them.* The CA should accept people in their environment. He must work in the home—he cannot accept the person only if he is clean, neat, polite, and obedient. He does not need to accept the conditions of the home in the sense that he must agree with them or like them, but he must learn to accept the person he visits in his home.

The visiting CA must communicate to the person and his family, for he is working now with the total family, not just with the person with a problem, "I think I understand how you feel since I am trained to understand problems. I think I can help you, at least I want to try. I will try to be perfectly honest with you and I will level with you at all times. I will keep my word with you. I will keep your confidences. I will not make fun of you or laugh at you." Something of this nature appears to be at the root of an honest, trusting relationship. The CA says in effect, "I do not think ill of you for having this problem. I do not look down on you nor do I think that I am better than you are. I think you are a worthwhile person and that you have capabilities for handling your own situation."

If the CA himself can be accepting and trustworthy, then the prediction is that the family in turn will respond in the same way. It is difficult, if not impossible, to make others accept or trust you. It would appear that people trust as they are trusted and accept others as they are accepted.

A trusting relationship is not built all at once. It seems that the level of trust is continually being

tested, and it continues to grow or to diminish as we work at the other conditions. The CA works at his task of treating the problem conditions, and while he works he builds the relationship with the family. These two vital activities are going on simultaneously. He must work at them both together.

Data Flow

The amount of information that is shared between the CA and the family is a function of the level of trust that has been established, according to this model. If the CA sees the person and the family as being stupid, unfriendly, uncooperative, disinterested, uninformed, then he is not likely to share very much information with them. The reverse is also true. If the family members see the CA as unconcerned, unfriendly, unaccepting, and not trustworthy, then they will probably tell him very little of how they really feel, what their real concerns and problems are. One CA was heard to say, "How can I get people to tell me the truth? I ask them questions about their activities, and I know they are lying to me." One would predict that the level of trust between the CA and the family is not at an adequate level. It would appear that the individual or the family feels that if they tell the CA the truth he will punish them in some way, or think poorly of them, or "bawl" them out. When people hold back information or distort the data, it is usually because they are not confident and secure in their relationships with the persons with whom they are communicating.

CAs are caught in a dilemma in the area of sharing data, for here it seems that openness begets openness of communications. CAs often feel they cannot tell all they know or suspect, for they fear they will lose contact with the family if they say too much. Indeed, all CAs are aware of situations where the CA has been severely chastised for talking too much. But such incidents sometimes lead CAs to be overly cautious — too reluctant to communicate with the person and his family. If there are areas that should not be discussed, the CA should frankly say: "This is an area I am not to talk about according to my own personal or professional standards. You must take this up with the person trained to deal with these questions."

People watch very carefully for the reactions of others to their communications. If a family member tells the CA how he feels about his situation or about another person and senses by observing the raise of an eyebrow or a facial grimace that the CA disapproves, this will often set the limit of the communication flow. CAs especially need to be aware of their reactions to others and how others perceive them.

Some interesting norms have developed in the helping professions about the sharing, or rather the nonsharing, of certain kinds of data. In some circles, it is considered improper for a CA to express grief, sympathy, or deep concern. It seems that the basic idea is that it seems inappropriate for the CA to wallow in self-pity. But CAs may be able to express real feelings and emotions without giving themselves up to emotions that would not be helpful to others.

The fundamental point here is that problems and situations can be dealt with only to the degree that we know about them. If people are holding back information, the CA cannot really do his job. If they are afraid of the CA, then they will not share all of the data with him. He must build the type of relationship which has enough basic trust that all of the data relevant to the situation can be freely discussed; all feelings, reactions, and concerns can be openly and honestly dealt with. Goals can be set and decisions made only within the realm of the data available.

Goal Setting and Decision Making

In the dependency-building strategy, goals are established by others and imposed on those below them, and decisions are made and the dependency-oriented person abides by the decisions made for him. It would not be surprising to find that in this type of situation there is a low level of commitment to the decisions made and the goals established. A wide range of research data reinforces the principle that commitment to a goal or a decision is directly related to the amount of involvement the people have had in the goal-setting or decision-making process.

In the CA-family relationship, the CA is profoundly concerned with having the person committed to the goal of improving. Often the CA is committed to this goal, but the person is not. When this occurs, the CA often moves to a process of imposed control, trying to coerce, plead, beg, browbeat, threaten, or in some other way, force the family member to follow through in the process of improving. One would predict that if the family member is personally committed to the goal of improving that he will take the responsibility himself for following proper procedures for his development.

And even within the general process of improving, there are a whole range of decisions that must be made. The model we are examining suggests that the family member and his family should be involved in making these decisions. Again, we often find that the CA has decided that this is good for the family, has really imposed this decision on the individual and the family, and then cannot understand why they don't follow this out. He says to himself, "Don't they know what is good for them?" The answer to this question is often, "No, they don't know what is good for them, but they may not be sure that the CA really knows what is best." They may be quite reluctant to blindly follow his program, particularly if there is a somewhat suspicious and nontrusting basic relationship and the CA has communicated very little to them about why he is doing what he is doing.

Some experience in watching the goal-setting, decision-making processes with groups of people suggests that these are not always fixed and immutable operations. Some people like to relook at decisions and reexamine goals, to rethink them and get a new commitment to them. Others like to make the decision once and then move ahead; they cannot understand the former type of person and often become

"Don't they know what is good for them?"

impatient with him. The CA may find all types of persons with whom he works — some may need to frequently stop and look again at their goals and decisions and really work through the whole process again. Others will make the decision once and move consistently ahead. The CA himself needs to be flexible and allow the family system to follow the best goal-setting, decision-making procedures.

This whole process suggests that the CA must spend time helping the family system (this includes all involved persons — usually the total family) work through setting goals and making decisions about better family practices. This takes time and is often a bugaboo for the CA who is usually overloaded. It is easier and less time-comsuming for the CA to come into the home, appraise the situation, make the decisions, and then tell the family what to do, coming around from time to time to check up and see if they are doing what he has told them. In a real sense, the CA has "taken over." The problem here is that the family is the one that should take over. If the CA is going to terminate the case and feel assured that the family is capable of handling its own situations, then the family unit must take over its own development. When the CA takes over, this is usually the beginning of a dependency relationship, or a counter dependency relationship where the CA has a constant fight on his hands.

Control

This condition has already been alluded to in the previous discussion. The type of control that is used develops out of the three prior conditions. An imposed control system follows almost automatically from the general dependency/counter dependency strategy. We almost have to check up on people and use devices and pressures of various kinds to ensure consistent performance if we are the ones who have made the decisions. McGregor (1960) has suggested that a control strategy really stems from some basic assumptions about people. If we assume that people are basically lazy, stupid, apathetic, irresponsible, then we must make decisions for them, for they are not really capable of making intelligent decisions; then we must follow through and see that they do what we have told them. This strategy and these assumptions are commonly found in parents.

The Gibb model predicts that if there has developed an authentic, trusting relationship, where the family system is free to share all of the data and where the CA has entered into a collaborative relationship with the family goals, then the control problem is basically solved. Self-control is the rather automatic end result of persons or systems having made their own decisions. They are committed to reaching their own goals. If such is the end result of the CA-family interaction, then the dependency problem is in large measure solved. The family system is now not dependent but mature, working with the CA.

The Family System

It should be remembered that the whole interaction of the CA is with the family system, not just with one person. The CA is building a relationship with the system, not just with an individual, if he is going to do his best work. All of the conditions mentioned apply to the family system. Overlooking this may be disastrous. All persons in the system whose behavior is going to be affected by a decision should best be included in the decision-making process.

References

Bradford, Leland P., Jack R. Gibb, and Kenneth D. Benne
    1964   T-Group Theory and Laboratory Method. New York: Wiley & Sons: 679-710.

McGregor, Douglas
    1960   The Human Side of Enterprise. New York: McGraw-Hill Co.

Parsons, Talcott, and R. Fox
    1958   "Illness, therapy, and the modern urban American family." in G. Jaco (ed.), Patients, Physicians and Illness. Glencoe: Free Press: 242-243.

Planning for change is a constant need in any organization. There are always certain conditions, results, and consequences that managers in the organization are trying to modify in one way or another. These conditions to be changed (hereafter referred to as *output variables*) are such factors as profit/loss, production, costs, wastage, absenteeism, turnover, apathy, involvement, quality, and so on. Whenever one of these conditions varies in an undesirable direction, steps are usually taken to try to improve things. The steps one takes to improve such outputs result from the diagnosis one has made as to what other factors are responsible for the drop-off in the output variable. The adequacy of one's diagnostic ability to think appropriately in terms of cause and effect will make a significant difference in the appropriateness of the action taken which then will influence the output.

If there is a poor diagnosis, it is probable that the action taken which is designed to improve output factors will result in inadequate change in the direction desired. Every organization manager — be it in business, government, volunteer organization, service organization, or in the home — has already developed some diagnostic schema. The presentation here will look at a model of three interlocking systems that effect outputs. Hopefully this may help to improve the quality of diagnosing and action taking. Table 1 shows that, according to this model, output variables are a result of three interlocking systems: the social system, the operation system, and the administrative system. Outputs are probably related in some degree to all three systems, but at a given time one system may be more responsible than the other. If such is the case, it is important that we try to take appropriate action in the dominant influencing system, or desired results probably will not occur.

The Social System

Every organization has its social world, that dynamic condition made up of people of different positions interacting with each other — talking, arguing, helping, deciding, solving problems — working in some way with each other, trying to achieve some of the goals of the organization and to satisfy some of their own personal needs. Every social system has some basic components:

1. *The climate.* Here we refer to the prevailing emotional state shared by members in the system; this may be formal, relaxed, defensive, cautious, accepting, trusting.

2. *The communication network.* There are formal and informal patterns about who talks with whom, when, how often, and about what.

3. *The status-role structure.* We will always see some type of division of labor, some people performing one type of function and others doing something else. Along with this certain persons have higher status than others, hence more power and usually more influence.

4. *The pattern of management.* Some people in

Table 1: Systems That Influence Organization Outputs

Social System	+	Operation System	+	Administration System	=	Organization Output
				Policy		Profit/Loss
Climate		Work flow		Wage-Salary		Production
Status role		Equipment		Promotions		Costs
Decision making		Location		Fringe benefits		Absenteeism
Management style		Physical environment		Hiring-Firing		Turnover
Values		Material		Raises		Commitment
Communication		Work arrangements		Budgets		Involvement
Goals		Schedules		Reporting		Apathy
				Auditing		Quality

the organization have the responsibility to work in superordinate positions relative to others, with the assignment to help subordinates with their work. A particular pattern or style of handling this superordinate action develops in the social system. This pattern develops at the top in an organization and tends to become a prevailing condition throughout the social system (Likert, 1961).

5. *Decision-making method.* Since a basic process in any organization is to solve problems and make decisions, a method for handling problem-solving and decision-making requirements gets established in the social system. This is closely linked to the pattern of management but also includes the degree that decisions are made by a few or many; the use of all relevant resources in problem solving; the creativeness of decisions; and the degree of commitment to implement the decisions.

6. *Values and goals.* Organizations differ in that various social systems in the organization will identify certain factors as being more important than others and will place a higher value on some factors. Some of these valued items will become ends toward which effort is expended; these become the goals in the system. Social systems differ in terms of the things valued and the goals desired; how values and goals are established; and the degree to which members accept the values and goals and work toward them.

The Operation System

Every organization develops its method for getting work done — the unique arrangement of equipment, material, people, and the processes used to accomplish work. A common industrial operation system is the assembly line method in which men are arranged along a conveyor belt of some type, with the assembled product moving along the belt and each worker doing a specific task. The operation system can be altered by changing the equipment, using different basic or raw materials, arranging people differently, or

Every organization develops its method for getting work done.

changing the work assignments.

It is immediately apparent that the social system is deeply connected with the operation system, for the arrangements of people will affect their ability to communicate with each other. The work assignments and work flow will influence the pattern of management used and perhaps the ways decisions are made.

However, there are unique elements in the operation system that are distinct from the social system and can be altered separately, although some concomitant effects in the social system may be noticed. The operation system can be changed in any organization. A common university operation system shows a professor in a large lecture hall, standing at a podium in front, lecturing for a total period. If the class is broken up into small student groups, arranged in a circle, with the professor sitting in the circle, a different learning process is more likely to occur. However, if the professor is still afflicted with his notions of status and the role of the professor, he may still dominate the situation, still lecture, and still control the social system. For real change to take place some modification is necessary in both the operation and social system. But the professor in the large lecture situation will probably find it almost impossible to change the basic nature of instruction unless some changes are made in the existing operation system.

The Administrative System

Interlacing the social and operation systems is a network of policy, procedure, auditing, and reporting that represents a whole other system that operates in connection with the other two but somewhat separate. Every organization has established certain formalized procedures for setting down the standards, rules, and regulations that influence what happens in the other two systems. Some of the important elements of the administrative system are

1. *Wage and salary administration.* This sets

down the procedures by which pay levels are established and also outlines the ways that increases in salary are obtained or by which bonuses or special benefits are possible.

2. *Hiring-firing-promotions.* Each organization has some methods by which a person is hired into the organization and also criteria which establish the basis for terminating a person in the organization. Where advancement in position or change of status is possible, the administrative system outlines the procedures.

3. *Report-auditing.* Many organizations have some form of data collection on such matters as use of materials, finances, work output, and quality control. This usually takes the form of report taking or auditing procedures as a way of helping the organization determine what is happening to its resources.

4. *Fringe benefits.* More and more, organizations are establishing criteria and methods for allocating out the less direct rewards or fringe benefits such as leave time, vacations, sick leave, retirement, and insurance.

Organization Change by System Intervention

In the field of research on organizations, there are numerous examples of change attempts that have been made (some successful and some not) by altering some aspect of one of these systems.

The Administrative System

Perhaps one of the most common and easiest ways to try to invoke changes occurs in the administrative system. The old Hawthorne Studies describe attempts to change production by offering changes in the administrative system (Roethlisberger and Dickson, 1939). Workers in the Bank Wiring Room were offered a bonus if they would produce over the existing level of production, but production remained constant despite the offer of a bonus, or even when the bonus was eliminated. The observer, gathering data from the workers, discovered that in the informal

Every organization has methods for hiring and firing.

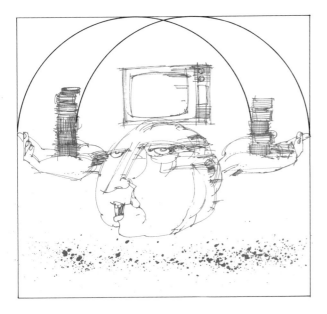

social system the workers agreed that if they increased production to get the bonus that either management would raise the base production level or management would see that fewer men could do the same amount of work and someone would be laid off. Since the existing situation was satisfactory, the workers agreed to maintain production at the existing level. It was also agreed that lower production brought tighter supervision; so a drop-off of production was not allowed. Informal sanctions were applied by the workers to each other when informal norms were violated. Thus an attempt to alter production by offering a bonus (a change in the administrative system) was not successful because of contrary conditions in the social system.

One management consultant described a situation where management in a production division became disturbed over obscene words written on the workers' rest room walls. It was agreed that this was a negative reflection on the company, and the strategy employed to eliminate this condition was to send a memo to the workers to the effect that this practice should stop immediately. New orders via memos are a common administrative method for inducing change. Evidently, the workers took this as a challenge, and obscene words increased. Management warned the workers that punishments would follow, but the words continued. A whole series of strategy-counterstrategy moves then followed. A monitor was placed in the rest rooms to police the situation, but this had no effect. Management was finally reduced to painting the walls every day at considerable expense and finally decided that the few obscene words they had at first were not worth all they were going through. All of the measures were stopped, and the words dropped down to the few that were there in the first place.

Most parents have tried the strategy of manipulating the administrative system as a means of inducing performance in children. In order to get children to study more, to practice a musical instrument, clean up their room, do their chores, parents will often offer greater rewards — such as larger allowances, more television — or will invoke penalties — such as no television or no allowance or no use of the car. This manipulation of the reward-punishment aspect of the administrative system in the home is reported by many parents as having limited positive effects.

The literature is replete with examples of experiments in altering the administrative system, trying to influence the organization outputs, with varying results. Manipulating the wage and salary conditions is a common strategy (Rothe, 1960:20-27). One study, for example, showed that when girls in an English factory who were threading needles for other girls to use were put on a piece-rate system (a change in the administrative system in an attempt to reward people who work harder) their production dropped from 96 dozen needles a day to 75 dozen a day. However, when the girls were told that when a girl reached a quota of 100 dozen per day the girl could go home, production immediately jumped and on the average girls reached their quota two-and-one-half hours early each day. Apparently, *money* incentives were not as important as *time* incentives for these girls, and an administrative change in the wage conditions was not as important as the time factor.

Apparently some improvements in organization outputs can be achieved by changing certain administrative practices, such as decreasing labor turnover by having better methods of personnel selection (Fleishman and Berniger, 1960:63-69).

However, in reducing accidents on the job, a study in a large tractor factory showed that the factor most highly correlated with accidents was the degree of comfort in the shop environment. Men who had to work in physically uncomfortable environments were most likely to become involved in accidents. Thus attempts to reduce accidents by signs, awards, and threats, apparently would not be as effective as making some change in the operation system (Keenan, Kerr, and Sherman, 1951:89-91).

The Social System

Ross and Zander compared employees who terminated their work situation with those who stayed and found a major difference came in the degree certain psychological needs were met. They state:

In this study we establish the fact that the degree of satisfaction of certain personal needs supplied by a person's place of employment has a significant direct relationship to his continuing to work for that company. These personal needs are for recognition, for autonomy, for a feeling of doing work that is important, and for evaluation by fair standards. In addition, knowing important people in the organization is related to continued employment (Ross and Zander, 1957:27).

The fulfillment of these needs is a direct consequence of what goes on in the social system. People are recognized, evaluated, and given a feeling of doing worthwhile work in a context of working with others in the organization. Some changes in the operation system might affect autonomy, but changes in the administrative system without some modification in the social system appear to have minimal effect. A great deal has been written about the effects of the pattern of management or supervision on organization outputs. This has been a major variable in research and is an important part of the social system. While supervision is related to productivity, the relationship, though still important, is surprisingly low. Argyle and his associates conclude: "The differences in productivity in work groups resulting from contrasting methods of supervision were typically small, usually not larger than 15 percent of the total output" (Argyle, Gardner, and Ciofi, 1958).

The management pattern has also been found related to grievances and turnover (Fleishman and Harris, 1962). This indicates that if one wishes to influence such organization outputs as productivity, turnover, and grievances, that one factor located in the social system is the pattern of management.

Dubin, in summarizing the work on supervision

and productivity, has this to say:

There is no "one best" method of supervision. As in all human systems, there is variability in the systems of supervision of industrial and commercial work. Several styles of supervision are effective, but they are individually successful only in relation to appropriate work settings. Variety in supervisory behaviors may no longer be considered a challenge to choose the "one best" for all settings, but rather as a challenge to understand where each does or does not work (Dubin, 1965:47).

Dubin in his analysis clearly feels that the type of supervision is related to the type of operation system. He describes differing operation systems such as unit production, mass production, and continuous production as differing kinds of operations that require alterations in management behavior.

In an extensive case analysis, Guest (1962) shows the effects on a manufacturing plant when the plant manager is changed. The new manager had a different style of management and introduced a number of changes in the social system, including regular report meetings where communications were opened to all supervisors in the plant. In addition, the new manager began to make a number of changes in the operation system by improving the physical comfort of the working areas, relocating ovens in the paint department, changing the number and length of conveyor lines in the trim department, and replacing outmoded tools. As a result of these changes in both the social system and the operation (with supporting administrative changes) the output variables were also changed remarkably — labor costs were reduced 14 percent; from being the highest of all plants in manufacturing costs the plant was 15 percent lower in manufacturing costs that the next best performer; absenteeism dropped from 4.1 percent to 2.5 percent and turnover dropped from 6.1 percent to 4.9 percent. In comparison to other plants this plant was one of the leaders in quality, safety, indirect labor costs, and grievances (Guest, 1962:98-103).

Another case study by Marrow and others (Marrow, Bowers, and Seashore, 1967) also describes the changes in output variables as a result of major changes in the management pattern. In this case a company was acquired and new changes introduced, especially new changes in the social system. The resulting analysis showed that performance of operators was improved. Changes in the operation system were also made, and some changes made in the administrative system. The authors conclude that the following changes were most important in the productivity of operators: (1) an earnings development program where individual counseling and help were given to individual operators; (2) the weeding out of low earners; (3) training in interpersonal relations for supervisors and staff; and (4) consultation and problem solving with groups of operators.

The authors (1967:183) state:

Although the technical changes at Weldon were on a large scale and affected nearly every employee, we find from our analysis that these changes cannot be shown to have improved operator performance.

It would appear that while items one, three, and four are changes in the social system, item two — the weeding out of low earners — is a change in the administrative system, that is a new change in policy about low earners.

Likert (1967) describes a study of management in the sales division of a large organization. He found that all of the top sales units in the division were characterized by managers who had a high supportive style of management, high performance goals, and a well-organized sales plan. Managers in the low producing sales units had low scores in both areas — supportive relations and performance goals. Likert feels that the presence of both of these conditions is necessary in the manager's behavior:

The preceding analysis shows that a manager who has high performance goals and excellent job organization but who relies solely on economic needs and direct pressure to motivate his men is very likely to be disappointed by their achievements. The non-economic motives must be used fully, along with the economic needs, to create high performance goals and establish the level of motivational forces which yield high productivity (1967:64).

The Operation System and Output

One of the strong exponents of the importance of the operation system in contributing to output variables has been Frederick Herzberg. He sees social system and administrative system variables as essentially *hygiene* factors — factors that remove hazards from the environment but which are not real motivators toward greater achievement. For him the motivators are in the nature of the job itself, and any basic change in motivation and hence output must come in some change in the nature of the operation system. He says:

Supervisory training in human relations is probably essential to the maintenance of good hygiene at work. This is particularly true for the many jobs, both at rank and file and managerial levels, in which modern industry offers little chance for the operation of the motivators. These jobs are atomized, cut and dried, monotonous. They offer little chance for responsibility and achievement and thus little opportunity for self-actualization. . . . A man who finds his job challenging, exciting, and satisfying will perhaps tolerate a difficult supervisor (Herzberg, Mausner, and Snyderman, 1959).

Herzberg (1968) describes the marked change in output variables (increased productivity, lower turnover, and absenteeism) in a work situation where girls doing routine correspondence were allowed to enlarge the nature of their work. Work had been done in a routine manner and was then modified to allow girls more control over their work and more responsibility for their own output. These modifications that lead to increased responsibility, challenge, and opportunity for growth are the real motivators according to Herzberg.

Motivation in the social system affects output.

McGregor (1967) recognized the importance of the operations system as it effects the organization outputs. He discusses three different studies all showing the effects on outputs by changing the basic operation of the work. In a coal mine in Britain, a textile mill in India, and an electronics firm in America the basic operation system was changed from individual workers doing a small specialized piece of the work to an operation system where workers functioned as a team in producing the whole product. In each case, productivity increased up to 30 percent.

There is a difference in making a change in the basic work flow and in making changes in physical conditions around the basic work operation. The Hawthorne Studies began with an experiment looking at the effects of illumination on productivity. In agreement with the hypothesis, as lighting got better, production increased. However, much to the surprise of the experimenters, as lighting decreased, production reached an all-time high. It became apparent that in the social system the workers felt they should work harder because they were part of an experiment, and it was the motivation in the social system and not lighting that affected the output.

Later in the Hawthorne experiments in the Relay Assembly Test Room, modifications were made in the operation system with the introduction of rest periods. Output increased markedly. However, in the last experimental conditions all rest periods were eliminated and production reached an all-time high. In analyzing the situation again, it appeared that production was more a function of building a close-knit social system than the alteration of the work with rest periods (Roethlisberger and Dickson, 1939).

Baveles and Strauss (Whyte, 1955:90-94) describe a situation in a toy factory where girls working in the paint section of an assembly line complained of the air circulation and asked for fans. Although the engineers claimed that fans would not help, they were still provided and production increased slightly.

Then the girls asked to have the assembly line conveyor controlled by two speeds — fast and slower and the right to regulate the belt to correspond with their physical reactions — to work hard when they felt fresh and slower when tired. This was also allowed and production improved sharply. However, the increased production from this section of the total assembly put pressures on work units on either side of the paint crew and they complained bitterly. Consequently, the management eliminated the modifications in the paint section. The foreman and many of the girls in the paint crew promptly resigned. This does point out the necessity of seeing the interlocking nature of the total operation system and how change in one part may affect other parts of the system.

One of the classic studies was done by Whyte in examining the restaurant industry. The existing work flow in certain restaurants shows that the operation system flows from the waitress taking the customer's order and passing the order directly to the cook, thus initiating work for him. Cooks were often responding negatively to lower status waitresses initiating work for them and would often frustrate the waitress by slowing down her orders. When the work flow was altered by eliminating the contact between waitress and cook by means of a spindle or a barrier between them and the orders passed in a written form, tensions and disturbances decreased (Whyte, 1948).

Perhaps it would be possible to reduce tension and conflicts between waitresses and cooks by working at the social system level — giving them some human relations training and helping them accept each other and work more cooperatively together. However, the alteration of the operation system appears to be more easily accomplished.

Principle of System Reinforcement

An examination of the above framework and the supporting research evidence leads to the development of the following working principle: To maxi-

mize output variables, all three systems (social, operation, and administrative) should function in such a way that they are mutually reinforcing. Table 2 identifies those conditions that seem to be necessary in the three systems to support desired organization outputs.

A social system that develops pride in the work group, mutual support, interdependence between management and worker, and high trust and acceptance is essential. An operation system, that keeps people isolated, working independently with no chance for interaction, and has controls for quality required by other than the workers, mediates against building the desired social system. If the above social system is desired, then an administrative system would *not* be supportive that required a checking up by supervisors, a tight audit and reporting procedure, secret reviews of performance, allocation of rewards determined by unilateral action by the person in charge, tight control of all expenditures only authorized by the top person, and little delegation of authority — only work assigned.

It is also extremely difficult to develop a creative and appropriate operation system or to revamp the administrative system, if the social system is not functioning well. If in the social system management is oppressive and controlling, decisions are not shared, communications are closed, trust is low, and people are highly dependent or rebellious, then the ability to work out new, creative procedures and work systems will be drastically reduced.

Persons who are trying to influence output variables are often not aware of the interconnections in the systems. One company was trying to carry out a new policy of decentralization. As the company grew, it became important to give more authority and autonomy to separate plant locations. Although the new policies gave more responsibility to the plant managers, top management for a number of unrecognized reasons did not allow managers control over capital expenditures. All expenditures over a

Social System	Operation System	Administrative System
• Workers are involved in setting goals and making decisions. • Open communications, people kept informed as to what is happening in the system. • High level of trust and acceptance. • Management is highly person-centered as well as concerned about production. • Management has high performance goals. • Workers feel needed, useful, doing something worthwhile. • Team spirit develops, and workers have pride in their work group. • Workers feel support, recognition from supervisors and others. • Workers experience "coaching" or help when needed. • Undue pressure is not exerted.	• Physical conditions are comfortable — do not require excess work, and safety conditions prevail. • Operation system allows workers time to interact with each other and build social support. • Workers are responsible for the quality of output of the operation system. • Workers have some control over the operation system; they are not entirely controlled by it. • Operation system requirements are matched to an adequate degree to the personal resources of the workers. • Workers have an opportunity to use a variety of skills and abilities on the job, as desired. • Operation system does not require too many conflicting interfaces.	• Rules and regulations are jointly established by management and workers when feasible. • Policies and procedures do not restrict adequate development of the social system. • Formal rewards given to appropriate management and worker behavior. • All benefits are distributed in equitable fashion. • Procedures and rules not inflexible, amenable to modification. • Workers involved in setting goals and doing work planning. • Restrictive reporting and auditing as control measures are not used. • Authority and responsibility are appropriately delegated. • Advancements and promotions result from open review between superior and subordinate.

few hundred dollars still had to be cleared with the executive committee. Until this policy was also changed, it was difficult to really achieve the goals of decentralization.

One of the increasing trends in industry is toward automation. This is a major alteration of the operation system. Such a drastic modification of work operations of necessity will require appropriate changes in the social and administrative systems. Some analysis of these trends has already been done (Whyte, 1957; Walker, 1957).

Summary

It has been proposed here that organization outputs are a function of the effects of three interlocking systems — social, operation, and administrative. To alter the outputs seems to require some modification of all three systems, at least a modification on one system should be supported by appropriate alterations in the others. It would appear that much of the current writing about Organization Development really seems to focus primarily on the changes in the social system. Likert writes about changing the organization from system 1 to system 4 (Likert, 1967) and is primarily concerned with changes in the social system. Social system analysis and strategies for change have come latest into the organization scene and have been given a great deal of needed attention. However, total organization development still requires a diagnosis of all systems that effect output with both sound diagnosis and appropriate change action occurring.

References

Argyle, Michael, Godfrey Gardner, and Frank Ciofi
1958   "Supervisory methods related to productivity, absenteeism and labour turnover." Human Relations 11 (February): 24-25.

Dubin, Robert
1965   Leadership and Productivity. San Francisco: Chandler Publishing Co.

Fleishman, Edwin A., and Joseph Berniger
   1960   "One way to reduce office turnover." Personnel
           37 (May-June): 63-69.

Fleishman, Edwin A., and E. F. Harris
   1962   "Patterns of leadership behavior related to
           employee grievances and turnover." Personnel
           Psychology 15:43-56.

Guest, Robert H.
   1962   Organizational Change: The Effect of Successful
           Leadership. Homewood, Illinois: Irwin-Dorsey
           Press.

Herzberg, Frederick
   1968   "Motivation, morale and money." Psychology
           Today 1 (March).

Herzberg, Frederick, B. Mausner, and B. Snyderman
   1959   The Motivation to Work. New York: John Wiley
           and Sons.

Keenan, Vernon, Willard Kerr, and William Sherman
   1951   "Psychological climate and accidents in an auto-
           motive plant." Journal of Applied Psychology
           35 (April): 89-91.

Likert, Rensis
   1961   New Patterns of Management. New York: Mc-
           Graw-Hill, Inc.

Likert, Rensis
   1967   The Human Organization. New York: McGraw-
           Hill, Inc.

McGregor, Douglas
   1967   The Professional Manager. New York: McGraw-
           Hill, Inc.

Marrow, A. J., D. E. Bowers, and S. E. Seashore
   1967   Management by Participation. New York: Harper
           & Row Co.

Roethlisberger, Fritz J., and William J. Dickson
   1939   Management and the Worker. Cambridge: Har-
           vard University Press.

Ross, Ian C., and Alvin C. Zander
   1957   "Need satisfaction and employee turnover." Per-
           sonnel Psychology 10 (Autumn): 327.

Rothe, Harold
    1960   "Does higher pay bring higher productivity?" Personnel 37 (July-August): 20-27.

Walker, Charles R.
    1947   Toward the Automatic Factory. New Haven: Yale University Press.

Whyte, William F.
    1948   Human Relations in the Restaurant Industry. New York: McGraw-Hill, Inc.

Whyte, William F.
    1961   Men at Work. Homewood, Illinois: Irwin-Dorsey Press.

Whyte, William F.
    1955   Money and Motivation. New York: Harper & Row Co.

Behavioral change agents engaged in management and organization development efforts recognize, as crucial, the solutions to the recurring problems of entry and transfer. The major feature of the project reported here and still under way is the attempt to optimize both entry methods and transfer activities by a single developmental approach, which includes the unique feature of using laboratory training to build a consulting relationship between internal consultants and their operating managers in an industrial organization.

The essential elements of the total design included (1) laboratory training as an initiating vehicle, (2) the use of internal Trainer-Consultants, (3) the use of data collection and feedback, and (4) a single management and organizational conceptual framework. A single framework was used to overlay prelaboratory, laboratory, and postlaboratory activity. Data about each of the twenty-five participating managers were collected from peers and subordinates prior to the laboratory. The laboratory allowed each manager to receive data from other participants, to receive data from back-home work peers and subordinates, to establish a working consulting relationship with internal consultants, and, with them, to begin to formulate a plan of action for back-home application.

Initial results from back-home application within the organization indicate that these design features have reduced the entry and transfer problems experienced in utilizing laboratory learnings in organization development. However, certain problems still exist in the transfer of learning, namely, uneven skill on the part of the managers to implement laboratory learnings, some lack of skill on the part of the Trainer-Consultants to intervene effectively, and the existence

*Revised. Reprinted by special permission from The Journal of Applied Behavioral Science, "A laboratory-consultation model for organization change," William G. Dyer, Robert F. Maddocks, J. Weldon Moffitt, and William J. Underwood 6 (1970): 211-23.

The problem of appropriate entry and responsibility is a recurring one for behavioral change agents.

of certain organization conditions that do not support change.

With the increasing number of organizations turning to management and organization development as avenues for increased effectiveness, two difficult problems have arisen as a real challenge to those engaged in such endeavors.

The first problem is mainly the result of organizations which place management and organization development in staff functions and hence confront the staff manager with the task of entry into the line organization. This problem of appropriate entry and responsibility is a recurring one for behavioral change agents.

The second and broader problem is that of the transfer of laboratory learnings to organizational improvement. Most of the attempts to do so can be subsumed under three models.

1. *The training model.* Managers can be sent to training programs geared to develop a motivation and conception for organizational improvement. Popular examples are Grid seminars, NTL Institute laboratories, and company-sponsored programs.

2. *The survey-feedback model.* Data can be collected about the organization and fed back to management as a basis for initiating problem solving. Examples are Beckhard's (1966) or Blake's (Blake, Mouton, and Sloma, 1965) confrontation designs and much of the survey action-research work of The University of Michigan (Mann, 1957).

3. *The process-consultation model.* A consultant can engage directly with a management group and use their ongoing business activities as a vehicle. Much of the development work at Esso R & E and Union Carbide Corporation serves as examples.

The Organizational Setting Prior to the Change Program

Recently, a method of combining desirable features from all three models into a single approach for initiating an organizational improvement project was completed by the Radio Corporation of America (RCA) training group in conjunction with two external consultants. The enthusiastic response of management and the training group suggests its usefulness to those working in the organization field as well as to those more specifically concerned with the issue of transfer of training.

RCA is a large international organization of some 120,000 employees engaged in manufacturing a variety of products and providing services primarily in the field of electronics. The organization has a highly successful business image in terms of growth and financial return.

In the company there are two organization development (OD) persons at the corporate staff level, and out in the divisions are six experienced staff persons and five others who are less experienced. This makes a total staff of thirteen persons available for OD work in the company, but only eight staff members considered experienced in OD.

There was no sense of urgency in the company on the part of management or the OD staff for immediately beginning an organization change program. Certain conditions were identified as pushing for change, but the desire was to build an OD model carefully with thoughts toward long-range results rather than some immediate transformations.

Previous Work of the OD Staff

Prior to the beginning of the organization change program, most of the internal OD staff were thought of as trainers (i.e., persons who diagnose management and organization needs, design a training program for certain personnel, and then conduct the program). The strategy for change was the hope that such training programs would lead to a change in management performance and perhaps in the organization. The staff felt that the training programs they were conducting were not producing adequate transfer into the organization, and that a different model of change was necessary — including a different way for the OD staff to work with managers. Although the staff felt competent in training and felt comfortable with their knowledge of new methods of OD, they lacked experience in carrying out new OD programs, e.g., consulting, team building, intergroup building. The image that the managers saw in the OD staff was a trainer image; these were people who conducted training programs but did not work regularly and consistently in the organization with the manager. This image needed changing.

Features of the Change Program

For this project, laboratory training was chosen as an initiating vehicle. However, the problems of entry for the internal training group and of connecting the laboratory learnings with the organization were critical design issues. Recognizing the continuing problem of training transfer, the authors knew that some organizations provide internal consultants to serve as application resources to their managers who attend residential laboratories, while others use the "family" concept of composing the training group of managers who have ongoing working relationships.

It was within these experiences that the authors designed the RCA project and attempted to optimize both entry and transfer by a single approach. The essential elements of the design included (1) the use of internal Trainer-Consultants, (2) the use of a single management and organization conceptual framework, and (3) the use of data collection and feedback.

Internal Trainer-Consultants

The key factor in the total design was the utilization of a corps of full-time internal Trainer-Consultants (presenting the trainer image mentioned above.) The individuals used were RCA division training staff who carried the training responsibility for managers in their organizations. This group was to form the major link between the training laboratory and back-home organizational application. The Trainer-Consultants (hereafter called T-Cs) had been attempting to establish a working, consulting role with management as a supplement to their normal training activities. However, at the time this project was conceived, the consultant-manager relationship had not been fully developed. It was decided that this project would be used to build such a relationship and that this relationship would be the instrument for back-home application. The T-Cs would be expected to follow their managers back into their organizational units and to continue to find ways of transferring laboratory learnings into the organizational setting.

It was decided, therefore, that the laboratory would be restricted to only those managers who would be willing to come to the program with their respective internal T-C and who would commit themselves to working with him prior to, during, and following the laboratory experience. A description of the proposed development project was discussed with a select group of managers who, in the past, had indicated a desire to initiate development activity within their organizational units. All twenty-five managers who were invited agreed to participate in the project.

It was necessary to build a set of conditions within the laboratory which would enable the consultant-manager relationship to be established. One requirement, therefore, was to bring the T-Cs and managers into contact during the laboratory in such a way as to establish an open and trustful relationship similar to the one which often develops between laboratory trainers and participants.

The design must also allow the T-Cs and managers to share the learnings of the laboratory, thereby cementing the consultant-manager relationship and avoiding the blocks that often appear when two people have to work together on issues which have not been shared in a common experience. This is particularly important since an effective consultant-manager relationship can be blocked by forces in the organization.

Since establishing a working relationship would also require that the T-Cs be seen by their managers from the beginning as being an integral part of the laboratory, the design of the project called for the internal T-Cs to do the following:

1. Collect data prior to the laboratory about each of their managers from his subordinates and peers.

2. Consult with their managers during the laboratory regarding the experiences the latter were having in the laboratory itself and on the back-home data which were given to the managers at a precise time during the laboratory.

3. Develop the kind of relationship with their managers which would carry over to the organization.

4. Continue to work with their managers within their organizational units after the laboratory in order to design and implement a plan of action to move the laboratory learnings toward organization application.

Unifying Conceptual Framework

A second major design feature was the decision to provide a single unifying framework to the total project which would provide a cognitive map for the learning taking place in the laboratory and for relating laboratory learnings to the organizations of each of the participating managers.

The idea of a cognitive framework is not new. "We should always be sure in designing learning experiences that they have both confrontation and a support for current orientations built into them. Cognitive models have particular value in the analysis of problems of transfer of learning" (Harrison, 1965).

The idea of using a single framework to overlay prelaboratory, laboratory, and postlaboratory activity *is* new. We wanted to avoid the fairly typical response to laboratory learning, "I think I learned a lot, but I really can't say what it is or how it applies"; or the condition stated as, "Laboratory values are so different from the values of most organizations that if the individuals learned well while at the laboratory, they would probably tend to conclude that they should *not* use their new learning back home except

The idea of using a single framework to overlay prelaboratory, laboratory, and postlaboratory activity is new.

where they have power and influence" (Argyris, 1966). The choice of a single framework for simplicity and understanding but one that was broad enough to avoid oversimplification was seen as critical. Likert's (1961) system of organizational characteristics, which arranges several behavioral categories into a matrix with four general styles, was chosen as an appropriate vehicle.

Data Collection and Feedback

Another important project element was the use of three separate data-collecting instruments. While each was geared to a different purpose, all three were designed under the Likert conceptual framework. The instruments measured behavior along the following dimensions: leadership, motivation, communication, interaction-influence, decision making, goals, and control. Measurements of each dimension were differentiated across four broad management styles, ranging from autocratic to participative.

One instrument was built to focus on the individual behavior of the manager in his organizational role. Each manager had subordinates and peers fill out this instrument just prior to the laboratory. Data were received, profiled by T-Cs, and held to be fed back to the manager at a certain point in the laboratory.

Another instrument was constructed for the dual purpose of assessing the processes of a T-Group and for assessing individual T-Group member behavior. The latter purpose provided the manager with systematized feedback on his behavior from this fellow T-Group members in the same conceptual framework used for the data gathered from his organizational subordinates and peers.

The third instrument designed for the project was cast at the organization level and built specifically to assess the processes of an organizational simulation exercise used in the laboratory. The use of this instrumentation was expected to meet several objectives, the most important of which was to aid learning transfer. The instruments appeared to be an effective method of illustrating the operational value of the management and organizational conceptual framework. Data collected under a common framework were expected to be useful in helping the manager relate his laboratory behavior to his organizational behavior. In addition to their transfer value, the instruments were expected to aid the laboratory learning process and to illustrate for the managers the feasibility and value of collecting quantitative data about human behavior and relationship processes.

These three key elements — internal consulting resources, a single conceptual framework, and data collection — were viewed as bringing together for this project successful approaches from prior experience in the fields of training and organizational improvement.

Preparing the Internal Consultants

Prior to the beginning of the laboratory, the seven internal T-Cs were brought together to prepare them for the laboratory experience and for their follow-up work with their managers in the back-home organizational application. During the two-and-one-half days thus spent, part of the time was used for giving the T-Cs an opportunity to contribute to the general design elements of the laboratory, since its preliminary design had been done by the outside consultants and two internal trainers. The design work completed to this point called for the internal T-Cs to have a major decision role in locating and prescribing the timing and nature of consultations which would take place between them and their managers.

The major role of T-Cs during the laboratory experience was to act as ongoing consultants to their managers. They were to observe their managers in all aspects of the laboratory — T-Groups, exercises, and theory sessions. They were to interact with their managers in a consulting capacity which would help them to function more effectively during the total laboratory experience. The week was to be used to

The major role of T-Cs during the laboratory experience was to act as ongoing consultants to their managers.

practice their consultation skills and to build the type of consultant-manager relationship that would be functional when they went back to their organizations.

The T-Cs were also briefed on the use of data. They were responsible for feeding instrumented data back to their managers. Time was spent in helping the T-Cs interpret data and in examining ways data could be fed back in usable form, so the managers could identify those characteristics in the Likert system relating to their managerial performance which required planning for improvement.

Time was also spent in talking about and role playing the building of the consultant role. A model of the consulting process was presented which examined the various dimensions of control. The T-Cs looked at the types of requests which could be made of them by the managers during the laboratory and the ways in which varying responses to these requests would result in the T-Cs either exercising control over the managers or allowing the managers more autonomy. The T-C saw that his function with his manager was to help the manager increase his awareness of the processes going on around him, to recognize the feedback given in the T-Group, and to begin to plan more effective behaviors for himself without relying on the T-C for direction.

The Laboratory Phases

By way of overview, the major phases of the laboratory design were as follows:

Overview

Phase I — 2 days. Concentrated T-Grouping focused on general personal and interpersonal issues. A day-long marathon was used on the first full day.

Phase II — 2 days. T-Grouping was combined with organizational exercises and theory sessions. The learning focus was shifted to group and organizational dimensions.

Phase III — 1 day. The collection, feedback, and

analysis of data. Managers were supplied with data from both their organizational colleagues and their laboratory colleagues. The learning focus was the manager's impact on others along managerial and organizational dimensions.

Phase IV — 1 day. Participants were assigned to use this period in whatever way they considered to be important. They chose concentrated T-Grouping, both to process their instrumented data with others and to resolve remaining issues developed in the T-Group.

Because these phases were intersected by the key elements previously described, the laboratory will now be described to illustrate the use of each feature in the program.

Phase I

During the concentrated T-Grouping in Phase I, the T-Cs took three roles. First, they acted as observers watching the behaviors of their managers as they interacted with others. Second, they met with their managers in three private consultations interspersed throughout this period. The initial consultation was used to clarify the purpose of the several consultation periods scheduled in the laboratory agenda. Generally, this was described as helping the manager obtain maximum value from the laboratory events. The remaining consultation periods in this phase were used to help the manager focus more deeply on his experiences in the T-Group. The third role taken by the T-C was to collect, tabulate, and feed back data. During the marathon on the first day, managers completed a group questionnaire designed around the Likert format. The results, in profile form, revealed to the managers that nearly all perceived their T-Groups to be operating somewhat autocratically but that each perceived himself to be operating more participatively. This brought into the design the features of the conceptual framework and data collection as well as opening up data for analysis in the T-Group.

Phase II

During the focused exercises on group decision making and organizational processes in Phase II, three more private consultations were scheduled. Each of these was held immediately following either an exercise or a theory session and in turn was immediately followed by a T-Group session. This scheduling gave the T-C an opportunity to help the manager assess his behavior in structured task work and to relate it to his behavior in the T-Group. These consultations tended to open for the manager new dimensions of concern which he could then test out in the T-Group.

Also during the second phase, the Likert-type questionnaire assessing organizational processes was used during the organizational exercise. For the second time the managers were exposed to the use of quantitative data by a replication of the conceptual framework, but applied to a different context.

Phase III

Phase III was used entirely to collect, feed back, and analyze data. First, each manager completed a questionnaire on every other manager in his T-Group. The questionnaire was designed within the Likert framework but geared to assess individual behavior in a T-Group. After each manager had received the results from his T-Group peers, he met with the T-C for help in analyzing the data. A T-Group session following this analysis was used for processing concerns raised by the data.

The final event in this phase was particularly significant to the entire design. It consisted of the T-Cs making available to the manager the profiled results of data collected prior to the laboratory from the manager's organizational subordinates and peers so he could assess the findings.

Thus, at this point the manager had available comprehensive data which included (a) systematized perceptions of his management behavior in his organization; (b) feedback he had obtained from the T-

Group and exercise sessions of the laboratory, and the analysis of this in previous consultations; (c) systematized perceptions of his T-Group behavior; and (d) the resources of a T-C.

The hazard of data overload was reduced by the single conceptual organization of most of the data and by allowing a considerable amount of time for processing in private consultation. The substantial impact of this event derived from the direct relatability of laboratory data to organizational data by the single framework. Plainly, the manager had considerable data about himself in relevant roles, and in what to him was management language. The T-C helped the manager relate the various pieces of data and make his own personal assessments.

Phase IV

In Phase IV the managers were requested to decide for themselves what activities would be most useful. They chose continuous T-Grouping. There were, therefore, no further consultations or data collections.

Application to the Organization

The first laboratory took place in May 1968. Since that time two more laboratory programs have been conducted which utilized the same design. Approximately ninety managers have gone through the change programs. After the first group, the next groups included the subordinates of those managers who had attended the first session, with the plan in mind of building a pool of persons with a common experience with whom the consultant could continue to work in the organization.

Initially, the T-Cs had no specific design for working with the participants back in the plant, except for a general notion of continuing the consulting started at the laboratory. However, it was discovered that practically all of the managers felt a strong desire to reveal to their subordinates something about their laboratory experiences, including data and analysis of the questionnaire ratings which the subordinates

Practically all managers felt a strong desire to reveal to their subordinates something about their laboratory experiences.

People were often embarrassed and uncertain about what to say and do.

had given them. It became the role of the T-C to help the managers plan and carry out such a communication process. Sometimes the T-C agreed to present the Likert framework in order to give the subordinates background and introduction to the data analysis.

Results of these meetings with subordinates have varied widely. Some managers presented the data, had a limited discussion, but did little follow-through for reasons to be discussed. Others used this as a base for continuing a set of problem-solving meetings to work on the issues raised by the data. As might be predicted, the meetings of a manager with his staff were characterized by the following processes:

1. *Initial Threat.* This was a unique experience for almost all of the persons involved. By and large the culture of the company did not have norms that supported such openness of discussion. People were often embarrassed and uncertain about what to say and do.

2. *Reluctance to Respond and Flight.* After the manager and/or T-C had reported the laboratory experience and data, subordinates were asked to respond. This invitation was met by reluctance and often by elements of flight behavior.

3. *Provisional Resolution.* If the units were able to deal with the first two conditions, an attempt to work out resolutions to problems raised followed. The units which decided to continue generally set up procedures and times to work on the issues raised in the early meetings. It was noted that the units that did not continue could not make decisions to work on their own staff problems. The continuing groups have gone in different directions: Some have initiated direct family T-Groups; some have used data collection-feedback sessions; others have stayed with the discussion of the original laboratory-generated data.

Continued OD Efforts

Results of the program have been determined by reports coming directly from the T-Cs working with the managers; systematic research designs have not been used. The direct reporting and anecdotal data indicate that about 25 percent of the managers who have participated in the three laboratories over a one-and-one-half-year period have *not* continued in any detectable OD efforts beyond the first meetings. Another 50 percent are continuing to make an effort toward OD, but the results are not considered totally effective by the T-Cs who are working with them. The remaining 25 percent have accomplished and are continuing to work on organizational change efforts that are considered significant improvements.

One manager who has been seen as particularly effective was perceived in the laboratory data as being very stiff and formal with his men; and, since he was younger in age than most of his subordinates, some real barriers were created in working effectively with them. His organization, a staff service to a production operation, was, up to that time, widely judged to be mediocre in effectiveness. As a result of the laboratory experience, the manager and his T-C began a series of team-building meetings which reduced the level of formality, rigid role differentiation, intellectualization, and one-way influence. As this manager's staff team changed, the effect spread to the other parts of the organization because of the renewed energy exhibited by his staff. Organization improvement in terms of hard data began to emerge. Recently this manager was given an unusually substantial promotion. He was placed in charge of a sizable plant that has experienced considerable difficulty. His superior acknowledged that a year before this manager would not have been considered for the new position, but the fact that he was able to change and was able to bring about an improvement in his organization gave them some confidence that perhaps he had learned how to bring about change in another problem situation.

Characteristics of Abortive OD Efforts

Where managers have not continued to develop

an improvement program, it has been felt that one or a combination of negative factors has been present in the following organizational components:

1. *The Manager.* Some managers have not seemed to benefit from the laboratory experience either for certain personal reasons or because their own anxiety about engaging in an open, leveling process with subordinates has been so high as to make further action difficult.

2. *The Organization.* It has become painfully evident that certain parts of the organization culture do not support continuing OD efforts. Sometimes the manager who went through the laboratory was faced with a boss who would not support new behaviors. Others found that work pressures requiring frequent travel, heavy overtime, and urgent time deadlines prevented the manager from moving ahead with the development meetings he would have liked to hold.

3. *The T-C.* It must be admitted that this is no "game" for a novice. Inappropriate interviewing or mistimed or inadequately handled interventions by the T-C have undoubtedly had negative effects. This issue is so sensitive that a single fault by a T-C has in some instances permanently blocked further OD efforts for some units.

Four models are now being used to engage the participating managers in development activity. These are (a) private consulting with the participating managers, (b) process interventions in regular business meetings, (c) direct and instrumented examination of staff teamwork in meetings established especially for this purpose both on and off plant premises, and (d) data collection and feedback from subordinates and other organizational members using a Likert conceptual framework to assess interpersonal data and as a data source for staff group action. (No T-C is engaged in private consulting with his participating manager as an exclusive process. Private consulting when used is being done in combination with one or more of the other processes.)

Critique

In reviewing the approach thus far, several weak and strong points can be identified. Two problems emerged during the laboratory, and another became visible during the application period, which is often the case.

Weaknesses

One problem concerns the number of managers worked with by the T-Cs. One T-C brought nine managers to the laboratory while another brought only one. The remaining ratios fell between these. Therefore, while in the one-to-one ratio team the T-C could spend a given time period in individual consultation, team ratios of more than one manager required the T-C either to reduce the individual time or work in subgroups. Although the design was timed to provide as much balance as possible, the consensus among the training staff was that more consulting time was available than the low-ratio teams could productively use and not enough time was available for the high-ratio teams. The optimum ratio for this design seemed to be about three managers per T-C.

Another problem concerned the use of one of the questionnaires. It was anticipated that collecting and feeding back group process information via the Likert framework during the first-day marathon would aid group development as well as introduce the framework and the use of quantitative methods. In fact, the managers displayed very little interest in these data, and it was not observable that the method had any effect, positive or negative. It is probable that such quantitative data were too "cold" to fit the context of the personal involvement of a marathon in a T-Group.

Another problem has become visible during organizational application attempts. A few of the managers, while highly motivated to apply, have defined change goals more in terms of others than of themselves.

Strengths

The entire project to date has yielded several results which are considered highly valuable. It is clear that a successful relationship has been built between the T-C and his managers. From all observations of the T-Cs, their managers see them as useful resources and understand the nature of their role; they are desirous of utilizing them as adjuncts in the manager's back-home application efforts.

As indicated, a majority of the managers have either initiated application activity or have voiced intentions of doing so. This is interpreted as a clear indication that the project has produced an intention to apply laboratory learnings. At this point, there is every reason to believe that training will be transferred to the job in significant ways.

With respect to the laboratory features which can be judged as helpful, the following appear salient:

First-day marathon. This up-front period of continuous and intensive T-Grouping was judged by the staff as moving the groups to a point approximating the third day of a standard laboratory design.

Single conceptual framework. The staff considered the use of a single overall framework to be quite useful. During the laboratory it provided a consistent set of dimensions which were inclusive enough to refer and relate most of the laboratory phenomena as well as organizational phenomena. This framework has continued to be highly useful as an organizing system for considering application goals and approaches.

Relating laboratory and organizational data. It was apparent to all the staff that having an opportunity to compare laboratory-produced data with data from their organizational realities was highly valuable for the managers. It provided a means of cross-validation and of relating similar concepts. It seemed a sufficient method for combating the typical tendency to compartmentalize laboratory experiences.

Cross-feed between consultations and other laboratory activities. The T-Group and focused exercises

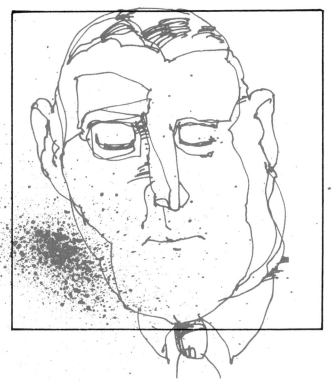

provided the data source for consultations; on the other hand, the consultations had a visible effect on managerial behavior in the T-Groups and focused exercises. Many a T-C observed his manager's explicit attempts in the T-Groups to explore dimensions which the consultations had previously exposed and dealt with. It is difficult to assess, but the staff impression was that private consultations produced a beneficial effect on the more traditional laboratory experiences.

Application Problems

In terms of organization application it seems that the Likert framework has given an expectation for and a focus on changing an entire organization. The managers have worked at the level of their own staff — a small-group orientation. They are impatient with the length of time which is seemingly required to change a total organization. We feel it important that the laboratory give the small-group element a greater emphasis and that it helps managers to see that the place to begin to influence the total organization is to improve group process within their own staff.

More attention needs to be given to careful selection of participants for the program. It seems that there are some types of managers located in certain kinds of situations for whom the laboratory experience can result only in minimal change efforts. If these can be identified, perhaps managers can be selected in whom greater possibilities for change are present.

It is our belief also that the laboratory should focus more attention on change strategies in addition to self-insight, and interpersonal group, and organization learnings. Managers who plan to engage in change efforts need to learn more skills, e.g., how to conduct confrontation meetings, data collection and feedback sessions, process analysis of meetings, team-building meetings, and so on.

Conclusion

The field of behavioral science interventions has developed a number of approaches to planned organizatioanl change. The one reported here has been a systematic attempt to utilize workable features from a variety of methods. It has been shown to be possible to build a laboratory design which incorporates internal T-Cs, quantitative data collection and feedback, and a single general conceptual framework into the more traditional laboratory experiences of T-Group, exercises, and theory input. The total approach, which has been evaluated as successfully facilitating entry into the organization and transfer of laboratory learnings into the back-home setting, hinges tightly on the continued use of an internal resource person.

References 213

Argyris, Chris
    1966   "Explorations and issues in laboratory education." Explorations in Human Relations Training and Research 3:15.

Beckhard, R.
    1966   "An organizational improvement program in a decentralized organization." Journal of Applied Behavioral Science 2(1):3-25.

Blake, Robert R., Jane S. Mouton, and R. L. Sloma
    1965   "The union-management intergroup laboratory." Journal of Applied Behavioral Science 1 (1):25-57.

Harrison, R.
    1965   "Cognitive models for interpersonal and group behavior: a theoretical framework for research." Explorations in Human Relations Training and Research 2:109-110.

Likert, Rensis
    1961   New Patterns of Management. New York: McGraw-Hill, Inc.

Mann, Floyd C.
    1957   "Studying and creating change: a means to understanding social organizations." in C. M. Arensberg, S. Barkin, W. E. Chalmers, H. L. Wilensky, J. C. Worthy, and Barbara D. Dennis (eds.), Research in Industrial Human Relations. New York: Harper & Row.

Index

216

218